Sean Szeps is the funniest dad i[...] his mom says. A podcast host, writer and content creator, Sean is most well-known for his accidental advocacy, which arose from sharing his journey as a gay husband raising boy-girl twins.

Originally from America, Sean moved to Australia and began hosting parenting podcasts like Spotify's *The Dad Kit* and Mamamia's *The Baby Bubble*, both of which quickly garnered a cult following. This opened doors, allowing him to write about the queer parenting experience for outlets such as the ABC, Mamamia, Kidspot, *AdWeek* and *The Daily Telegraph*.

As a passionate advocate for the LGBTQIA+ community, Sean launched Australia's first-ever coming out podcast, *Come Out Wherever You Are*, with SCA's LiSTNR, his guests including Billy Eichner, Courtney Act, Abbie Chatfield and Patricia Karvelas.

Sean lives in Sydney with his husband, Josh, and their twins, Stella and Cooper.

Not Like Other Dads.

A fearless, frank and funny memoir about reinventing the rules of parenting

Sean Szeps

ABC
BOOKS

This is a work of non-fiction, but in some instances I have found it necessary to change names*, mostly because I was sleep deprived and can't remember.

This book contains sensitive themes. If it raises any issues for you, you can contact Lifeline (13 11 14), Beyond Blue (1300 22 4636) or QLife (1800 184 527).

 The ABC 'Wave' device is a trademark of the Australian Broadcasting Corporation and is used under licence by HarperCollins*Publishers* Australia.

HarperCollins*Publishers*
Australia • Brazil • Canada • France • Germany • Holland • India
Italy • Japan • Mexico • New Zealand • Poland • Spain • Sweden
Switzerland • United Kingdom • United States of America

HarperCollins acknowledges the Traditional Custodians of the land upon which we live and work, and pays respect to Elders past and present.

First published in Australia in 2023
by HarperCollins*Publishers* Australia Pty Limited
Gadigal Country
Level 13, 201 Elizabeth Street, Sydney NSW 2000
ABN 36 009 913 517
harpercollins.com.au

A catalogue record for this book is available from the National Library of Australia

ISBN 978 0 7333 4269 1 (paperback)
ISBN 978 1 4607 1560 4 (ebook)

Cover design by Mietta Yans, HarperCollins Design Studio
Author photograph by Stacey Rolfe Photography
Typeset in Bembo Std by Kirby Jones
Printed and bound in Australia by McPherson's Printing Group

To anyone who's raised a tiny human and felt lost along the way, this one's for you.

Contents

The Prologue

It all started with a teapot. I was four years old and watching Disney's *Beauty and the Beast* for the first time. I didn't plan on hero-worshipping a piece of kitchenware that day, yet that's exactly what happened. Belle was likeable, and I've never met a seven-foot-tall hairy man I didn't fancy, but it was Mrs Potts who won my heart. She was nurturing, reliable and direct. She efficiently ran the castle while raising her son and parenting the rest of the staff, and she successfully plotted to bring the Beast and Belle together in the end. Although I was barely capable of spelling my name or feeding myself, I knew right then that I wanted to be like her. I wanted to be a mother.

From then on, most of my on-screen role models were women with children. At the age of seven I moved on from Mrs Potts to Didi Pickles in *Rugrats*, an animated TV series. She was a hands-on mom who juggled a career as a psychologist with supporting her absent-minded husband. Sure, she was a little obsessed with parenting 'by the book', but she put her family

1

first and that resonated with me. When my younger brother, Steven, began worshipping Buzz Lightyear from *Toy Story*, I was busy fixating on Carol Brady from *The Brady Bunch*. She was fashionable and funny, a fierce stay-at-home mother who took on an impressive list of extracurriculars without ever missing a family dinner – a feat much more impressive than Buzz's hand-to-hand combat skills. As I grew older, the trend continued. Clair Huxtable from *The Cosby Show* and Kitty Forman from *That '70s Show* joined the matriarchal ranks, followed by Fran Fine from *The Nanny*, Becky Katsopolis from *Full House* and Carol Foster Lambert from *Step By Step*. They were avatars for the parent I hoped to be one day: powerful, kind and beloved by men.

Those fictional moms moved through their homes with effortless control, the Gorilla Glue that held their families together. Dads went off to work and made the money, but to me it was clear who really ran the show. Moms were the ones cooking, cleaning and organising the home. Experts at family admin, they were laser-focused on raising kind and respectful children, too. They were the ones who – as far as my television-viewing schedule was concerned – made sure their children turned out to be good people, a responsibility that rested on their shoulders alone. They cared about their kids on an aggressively empathetic level. If I'd been given a choice between becoming a mom or a dad, I would have been on Team Mom every time.

It didn't take me long to connect the dots and realise that my fictional love affair with mothers stemmed from a real-life obsession I had with my own. I was born in 1988 and spent my first ten years in Concord, the capital city of the often forgotten US state of New Hampshire. I grew up there with my brother, Steven, less than two years my junior, and my sister, Samantha, born two years after him. My father, Steve Gallerani, was a deeply committed husband and father who I affectionately called Popsicle. And then there was my mother, Sally.

I hate to brag – really, I do – but I was raised by a modern-day Mary Poppins. My multi-talented mom came from a long line of matriarchs; it seemed that motherhood ran in her veins. She didn't just cook: she was a chef. She didn't buy clothes, toys or Christmas decorations: she made them from scratch. She threw elaborate birthday parties that would have gone viral if the internet had existed. Her skills were far superior to those of most mothers I knew, but it was the joy that radiated from her – the genuine enthusiasm for the role of raising children – that really drew me in.

I was young when I made these observations, so I was blissfully unaware of the difficulty that the job actually entailed. On the surface, she seemed calm, cool and collected. She was the first and last face I saw each day, the warm embrace I longed for when things weren't right, and the answerer of questions when the world grew perplexing. If our family was a shirt, she was the hidden thread holding it all together. I wanted to grow up to be just like her.

It was impossible to ignore the way my father treated my mother. He worshipped the ground she walked on, and this had a big influence on me. He praised her parenting, supporting her every request without complaint. When he showered her with compliments – 'We'd be nothing without you, Sally. Thank you for everything you do' – it cemented the importance of her

This is my mother, Sally, with my brother, Steven, and my sister, Samantha. The stud with the bowl cut on the right is yours truly.

position. The importance of a mother. I wanted to have a family that was nothing without me.

I had other impressive real-life motherhood role models. My abuela, my mother's mom, was the Cuban Martha Stewart (minus the jail time). For most of my childhood she lived in the next town over, so we saw her frequently. I thought of her, in many ways, as a second mother. We always had a special bond. She took me back-to-school shopping, let me try on her antique sunglasses and taught me to appreciate art. I would stand by her side while she cooked, learning to master traditional Cuban cuisine. In the summer we spent a week at her house and called it 'Camp Abuela'. She would work with us kids to design and open a family restaurant that our extended family could visit at the end of the week. We researched cuisine online and developed a multi-course menu. We'd create a shopping list and group items by category to ease the purchasing process. We designed and printed elaborate menus on her computer, made table decorations, purchased flowers, decoupaged serving platters inspired by pre-selected themes, like 'Tour of Italy', and selected wardrobes that ensured we looked like Michelin star-worthy restaurateurs. My siblings and I mastered a handful of critical life skills, priding ourselves on our business savvy and mature use of etiquette at the end of the week.

My mimi, my father's mom, was a lifelong teacher whose empathy and understanding rivalled that of the Dalai Lama. She taught me about effective communication: how it's both an exchange of information and an opportunity to connect. When I was younger, she taught me about 'putting yourself in someone else's shoes' and 'doing your best to consider their needs and experience level, not just your own'. She taught me how to break down complex ideas into snippets that resonate with others, leaving our selves at the door to ensure that we can pass on our message to someone with a totally different perspective. It was by her side that I gained my superpower: an obsessive consideration for others.

This came in handy, as I was one of the oldest of many cousins. I was much more passionate than other kids my age about caring for younger children. By the time I was ten, I had mastered the arts of changing nappies and resettling babies. I knew how to warm milk bottles, defuse crying infants and use a nasal aspirator to clear a stuffy nose. As soon as I was old enough, I pursued babysitting as a money-maker.

When I was thirteen I began watching neighbourhood children in exchange for cash, racking up an impressive list of clientele. Before I arrived at my first job, my mom helped me design and print a checklist that I could complete with the parents upon arrival. Those simple questions not only made my job easier but also won over their trust within minutes: 'Where will you be and for how long?' 'How can I contact you?' 'Where's the first-aid kit?' 'When is bedtime?' 'Is television okay?' 'What are the house rules?' Mom also helped me pull together an activity list I could use if the kids got bored and I needed a bit of inspiration.

After I turned fifteen, the success of my babysitting business helped me get a job at the local after-school program. It was there that I accepted a one-on-one position watching a young boy with autism. My determination to learn how best to communicate with him – I learned basic sign language for the job – inspired me to want to study Child Psychology and maybe even get a minor degree in American Sign Language. This job also inspired me to become a full-time nanny during the summer before I left for college.

Working as a professional 'manny', I got my first real taste of parenthood. I would arrive before the kids woke up and stay with them until around 6 pm, often working twelve-hour days. I would get them out of bed, help them get dressed and make them breakfast, then I'd drive them around to various activities, make them lunch and take them shopping. Over the course of two summers in a row, including my first summer home from college, I became deeply invested in their well-being. I would help to throw birthday parties and plan outings with friends. Because their parents were very busy, I started to take personal ownership of their happiness. When it was time for me to go back to college my sophomore year and I had to say goodbye, I cried the entire drive home. I felt, for the very first time in my life, like I understood the power of the caregiver–child bond. I'd got a teeny-weeny taste of motherhood and knew I wanted more.

All of this is to say that I had more passion, more experience and many more mothering skills than the average teenager did. I was on a natural path to motherhood, perfectly prepared to help raise the next generation of Gallerani children. But there was a problem, a roadblock that would undoubtedly stop me from achieving my objective of becoming the world's most impressive mother: I was a man.

Chapter One

The Closet

When I was sixteen, I accidentally got a girl pregnant. Okay, that's not entirely true: I *thought* that I got a girl pregnant, and it wasn't really an accident.

My girlfriend met me at the entrance to our high school. It was obvious that she'd been anxiously waiting for me, hovering in the lobby, because I'd barely stepped foot inside before she grabbed my arm and whispered, 'I'm late,' into my ear.

'We have ten more minutes,' I replied, thinking she was talking about class.

'No, *late*-late,' she shot back. 'I was meant to start my period like seven days ago.'

We had been having sex for a few months, mostly with a condom. The last time we'd done the deed was the first time that I, you know, actually delivered the goods. After dozens of nervous attempts, my penis had decided to show up to the party. And now, minutes before I was supposed to walk into my World History class, here she was, my beautiful girlfriend, staring me in the face and informing me that I was about to become a sixteen-year-old father.

She's pregnant, like, for real, I thought to myself. *You need to tell your parents immediately. They'll be completely pissed … or maybe relieved? Definitely relieved – this will prove you're not gay. You should probably propose before you get grounded, and then buy a house. Do high school students who become parents and don't have any money buy houses? You'll need to get a big kid job with big kid benefits or double your hours at the cinema and work more weekend shifts at the ice-cream shop. You'll definitely have to drop out of the school musical, which is a bummer because this is your first lead. Actually, you'll need to drop out of school entirely. And then, you know, start thinking about baby names.*

My girlfriend's voice shattered my internal monologue. 'Are you paying attention, Sean?'

'Of course. Yes, sorry. This is just a lot to take in.'

If I'm being completely honest, I don't remember how the rest of that conversation went. I'd like to think I handled it with maturity – that I said something like, 'How can I best support you?' But I'm fairly confident I replied with something more like, 'Fuck. Have you taken a pregnancy test?'

My girlfriend ended up not being pregnant, and I ended up not being straight.

The 'pregnancy' was a bit of a wake-up call for me. In the three days between receiving the news and hearing the Maury Povich-style 'You are not going to be a father' announcement, I realised I wouldn't be able to hold on to the sexuality secret that I had been keeping from everyone – myself included – much longer. I knew that I liked women, just not in a sexual way. But I refused to look myself in the mirror and say the word 'gay' out loud. I wanted to be a parent and being gay would stop that from happening. I had to either suppress the truth or give up on fatherhood. I wanted fatherhood more than genuine happiness, but the thought of having to lie for a lifetime about my sexuality, to absolutely everyone, seemed unbearable.

Prior to that week, whenever I'd put my motherhood fantasies aside and tried to accept the reality of becoming a parent in modern society, I'd only ever thought about being a closeted father. I was living in fight-or-flight mode, doing my best to mask my sexuality so I could survive. As a practising Roman Catholic, I knew that being gay was one of the ultimate sins. I believed that if I came out of the closet, I would face a life of loneliness followed by death from AIDS and then eternal torment. It felt like my only option was to build relationships with girls based on strategic lies.

When I looked into my girlfriend's eyes the day after we learned she wasn't pregnant, I finally saw her – not as a supporting character in my movie but as the ingénue in her own. I saw her as a mother caring for a baby with a closeted husband. I imagined her learning, years later, that I had been having an affair with a man I'd met online. I imagined her having to tell our kids that their father was gay. And those thoughts made me physically ill. I realised I had been manipulating girls for my own benefit without thinking about the detrimental impact this could have on their ability to love or trust again.

When the churning in my stomach subsided, I was left with an unexpected feeling that was even more painful. I was jealous. I wanted what she could have. I wanted to be pregnant. I wanted to tell my boyfriend that I was having his child.

It was then that I understood what I had to do: I had to end the relationship and come out of the closet. But I was way too afraid to rip the Bandaid off entirely. What if God randomly heard my prayers and decided to gift me a delayed fondness for vaginas? I decided to ease my way into gayville. Bisexual today and gay – maybe – some other day.

★

I held in my hands a concise coming-out letter, one I had rewritten late at night about two hundred times. Each time I'd imagine which words might throw off my mother or trigger a cry. For many months, without fail, I'd find a flaw. I'd tear the page in half, then in half again, until I had a pile of tiny scraps on the edge of my bed. I'd scurry to the bathroom and wet the scraps, watching as the blue ink bled down the drain and the paper turned to mush. I'd slowly pull apart the damp snowball and deposit its pieces around the house: one piece down the toilet, another in my bedroom garbage can, a third down the kitchen sink, and the last one out my window into the backyard. Once the evidence had been destroyed, my anxiety would settle. I'd start writing the letter again, again and again and again.

But this time, on this night, the letter was perfect ... well, as perfect as it was ever going to be. After listening to Avril Lavigne's *Let Go* from start to finish – an album I decided had been created specifically to support me through this momentous occasion – I decided it was time. No more stalling, no more excuses: tonight, I'd come out to my mother.

I paced the hallway between my bedroom and my parents'. After a few hundred laps, I placed my right ear against their door, heard absolutely nothing and knocked twice with the nervous knuckle on my right hand. 'This is it,' I whispered under my breath. I grabbed the door handle, twisted it gently and pushed. A bright light was shining from the left side of their bed, my mother's side. She was awake and sitting up, just as I had hoped, the top of her glasses poking out above her laptop screen.

My father was asleep by her side – total relief.

I loved my dad. We had inside jokes, a secret handshake, and food that only we ate together. When he was driving me anywhere, he demanded that we listen to oldies, and with each new song he'd turn to ask me, 'Who sings this?' Over many years I became a connoisseur of 60s, 70s and 80s music, and this inspired my lifelong passion for singing. So my father and I had a strong connection. But, he wasn't my mother. He was kind but also quiet, masculine and reserved. If something was going to go wrong during this coming out to my parents experience, I thought it would most likely be with him.

Mom was the one who could help me. She was the one who needed to know that I was bisexual, until proven otherwise.

I walked over to her, my perfect letter beginning to rip as my right hand fiddled with its delicate edges.

'Is everything okay, sweetie?' Mom asked, setting her laptop on the bedside table.

I couldn't speak, not a single word. Every anxious thought, every lie, every prayer, every built-up fear that my sexuality would send me on a one-way trip to Hell had led to this very moment. I felt hot, sweat beading on my forehead. I found it impossible to look her in the eye, my gaze locked on the carpet. My body was trembling with an almost uncontrollable desire to run.

I handed her the letter containing my partial truth. I knew the letter was only fifty per cent honest, but it was an opportunity for me to gauge her reaction. Maybe I'd be a successful bisexual, marrying a woman but figuring out a way to get my kicks on the side. I wasn't sure how she was going to respond, but I was hopeful it would all be okay. Hopeful that my mom, the woman who had birthed me and loved me unconditionally my entire life, could somehow take away this terrible pain. Hopeful that when the words leaped off the page, my anxiety would melt away.

As Mom read my letter, she pulled her legs out from under the sheets and turned to sit on the edge of the bed.

My father snapped out of his deep sleep. 'What? What? What?'

Shit, I thought.

'Is everything okay, buddy?' he asked me.

I still couldn't respond. I stood there in silence, staring at my mom and only my mom. The emotions became too strong to hold in, and tears streamed down my face.

Then my mother finished reading, or maybe she didn't need to. As though she was throwing a rope in to rescue me just as I began to drown, she gently took me by the arm and pulled me next to her. She gave me a tight hug and whispered into my ear, 'Everything is going to be okay.'

In an instant I was a small boy again, warm in Mom's embrace, carefree and calm. For years I had forced a distance between us out of fear of disappointing her. But her love, her unwavering love, brought us back together. *If only I had told her sooner,* I thought.

My mother said, 'We love you so much, and nothing will ever change that.'

And my father, clearly uncomfortable with the whole situation, looked at me across the bed, gave me a sort of half smile and said, 'We've always known.' That was it: as soon as the three words fell from his mouth, he rolled over and went back to sleep.

My father was, and still is, a very traditional man of his generation. He hated when we swore or when our outfits were too wild by his standards. Dad would ask if I had a girlfriend but then add that he 'didn't need all the personal details'. He was known for long bouts of silence even among close friends, so I shouldn't have expected more from him. I'd hoped that his response would surprise me – that he would say something so profound that it would forge a stronger connection between us. That didn't happen, but back then his lack of an emotional response seemed way better than a slap to the face. It would take me weeks to wish he had said more, months to realise how hard it must have been for him, years to consider what he must have thought my sexuality would mean for my life, and nearly a decade to muster up the courage to talk to him about it.

But that night, I was just relieved that I had what many teenagers did not. A mother who loved me no matter what my sexuality was. A family member who was committed to my happiness. Someone who could take a small portion of the burden off my shoulders and onto hers. At that moment, I felt free.

*

Soon afterwards I dropped the 'bi' in 'bisexual' and replaced it with 'homo', officially coming out as gay to little fanfare in the year before I graduated high school. During that year, I made what I thought was an important observation: for a gay American man who didn't want to co-parent with a female friend or an ex-wife, nurturing dreams of fatherhood seemed like a waste of time.

I had tried googling, 'Can gay men have children?' and similar questions, and yes, it was possible. In the US, the first prominent example of a successful path to gay parenthood was singular: as in, one man in one state had adopted one child in 1968, and he'd said he was straight. Then there was the story of a gay couple in California adopting a child back in 1979 after battling with the courts and paying a bajillion dollars. None of it seemed easily achievable: marriage equality was still illegal, and it appeared as though the judicial system was not on our side.

I decided to bury my parenting dream and my memories of wanting to be a mom. I did my best to forget about Mrs Potts and my other idols, along with my passion for working with children, my plan to study Child Psychology, and my desire to follow in my parents' footsteps. I was standing on the precipice of adulthood, and I felt like I finally understood what my future could hold. I was going to university to study theatre and dance. I would continue loving Halloween and Christmas and eating Chinese food while watching *Sex and the City* reruns. I'd move to a big city after college, collecting a large friendship group along the way. And I was never, not ever, going to be a father.

Over the course of the next few years, randomly, when I least expected it, I would think of the child who almost was. I could see my daughter – for some reason it was always a daughter – running through my family home while calling for her 'pop'. I daydreamed about rocking her to sleep in a hand-carved wooden cradle. I fantasised about opening presents with her on Christmas morning and having my Tio Eddy, my favourite uncle, pretend to be Santa Claus. I could see it all so clearly: screaming her name from the sidelines of a swim meet, cheering her on as she touched the wall first, high-fiving the other dads, and basking in the glory of my very straight, very successful life.

I learned to suppress my sadness and replace it with an anti-parenthood agenda. I mastered a stand-up routine that allowed me to change the subject while masking my anger and disappointment whenever parenthood was brought up. 'Me, a parent? You must have mistaken me for a straight breeder. Do I look like a heterosexual male to you? I'm sorry, but I don't like vaginas. Children are simply not for me. It's just that, how do I say this, I have so many plans that will conflict with raising children – like sleeping eight hours a night until the day I die. Speaking of dying, I'd rather die than spend all my money on thankless creatures. While you're rushing to school drop-off, I'll be dropping off my Porsche at the shop and hurrying away to a gays-only retreat in Mykonos.'

My comedy routine worked – the crowd almost always got the hint and immediately aborted their friendly mission. And the more I spoke the lies into existence, the more I believed them. Before I knew it, they became my truth.

*

I left home at eighteen and moved into my college dorm at the University of New Hampshire. It was August 2006, and I planned to study Musical Theatre. I was out of my small town, out of the closet, and onto bigger and gayer things.

My pool of potential suitors expanded from one to twelve. I got my first real boyfriend that year, an upperclassman from the swim team, but the relationship was short-lived. I quickly replaced him with my second real boyfriend, making up for lost time in the closet. His name was Andy, and he was also an upperclassman – clearly I have a thing for older men. Our love story isn't anything to write home about: he was getting over an ex by climbing on top of me, and I was willing to give any guy a chance.

When I think of Andy, I think of the fact that both our first and second dates were to see the movie *Happy Feet*. I also remember that while we were dating, in 2007, the governor of our state signed a civil union bill into law. It gave same-sex couples the same legal rights as straight married folks – except the right to legally call their relationships 'marriages'.

'It isn't full-on marriage equality,' Andy said to me one night as we squeezed into his twin-sized bed. 'But it's a step in the right direction.'

'Why would we want what they have?' I asked. 'Marriage is a religious trap – and please don't get me started on children.'

'Let's say we kept dating and decided, one day, to get marr– to get civil-unioned. If you got really sick, I would be allowed into the hospital room to care for you. Prior to this bill, it wasn't so black and white.'

**I started dancing when I was five to get to the ladies. Okay, that's not true.
I did it for the costumes.**

As I attempted to fall asleep with Andy snoring beside me, a tiny smile crept into the corner of my mouth. For the first time in years, I felt a glimmer of hope that maybe, one day, I might actually want to find myself in … a civil union. The gay tides were turning.

If Andy was by my side when I took the first step, then my best friend Joe was there when I took the first leap. Joe and I met that very same year in my dance class. My beloved teacher had selected a few of us to perform a new routine for the rest of the students. Joe, a recent graduate, dropped by to watch. When I saw him standing in the doorway, my gaydar pinged at his spiky black hair, thick chin-strap and sparkly booty shorts. I danced specifically to impress him. I had heard rumours about him choreographing large group performances of the very best dancers in the school at the end of year showcases, and I wanted him to notice me in hopes of being considered. I gave absolutely everything I had in that performance. Everyone applauded, and I knew I had killed it.

At the end of the class, Joe pulled me aside. 'Can I talk to you for a second?'

'Of course.'

'So listen. Everyone's obsessed with you, and for good reason – you've got great stage presence. But you have some work to do, and you probably won't be able to get it all done by just taking classes here. If you want to get better quicker, I dance here alone on Tuesday and Thursday nights. The janitor leaves the back door unlocked. Come and dance with me.'

It wasn't an invitation to star in his next group number, but I had come to college to become a better dancer, so I showed up the following Tuesday to learn from Joe.

And learn I did. I became a better dancer and a better person. Soon we were inseparable, dancing for a few hours each Tuesday and Thursday, then driving around our campus and to the beach. We smoked weed and harmonised to musical theatre tracks, and together we explored complicated ideas about gender, sexuality and religion. We had a lot in common, as we'd both grown up as closeted Boy Scouts in the same state at the same time.

In June 2008, we were listening to NPR in Joe's car when California issued marriage licences to same-sex couples as a result of the Supreme Court of California finding that barring them from marriage violated the state constitution. When Iowa and Vermont did the same in April 2009, and eventually our home state of New Hampshire followed in June of that year, Joe and I were together, too.

'Great news, right?' he asked me as we drove to his favourite beach for some late-night stargazing.

'It's definitely not *bad* news. But I can take it or leave it. I'm not planning on getting married or having kids.'

'Because you don't want to or because they wouldn't let you, so you've buried the desire somewhere back in your childhood?'

Joe never beat around the bush. If he smelled even the slightest whiff of inauthenticity, he'd call you out on it. I didn't always enjoy his candour, but in this instance I knew he was right. I turned to him, a bit embarrassed, and said, 'Maybe it's the latter?'

'Maybe,' he replied, his eyes on the road. 'And I'm here to talk about it when you've figured it out.'

Little by little, right in front of my eyes, the world was changing. But I had spent so much time suppressing my feelings about one day being a parent, while developing the persona of a gay man who was happy without the possibility of having kids, that I honestly didn't know what I wanted anymore. I knew I'd be a great husband and a great father, but would the world be great to me in return? I still felt like the answer was 'no'.

At college I had joined a beautiful queer community led by Joe and my roommate Kristopher, who quickly became another of my very best friends. Meanwhile, I fell madly in and out of love with two wonderful men, Joshua and Michael. It was by all of their sides that I learned to love being gay, seeing for the first time that it wouldn't hold me back the way I had once thought it would. But if you can't see yourself, it's impossible to be yourself. Even though I'd been experiencing great love and friendship with wonderful gay men, when I prepared to graduate college in 2011, I looked out into the world beyond our campus and just couldn't imagine things changing for me as far as parenthood was concerned.

It was going to take a lot more than a few governors signing marriage equality bills for me to unpick the trauma of my closeted childhood. It was going to take something – or someone – very special for me to imagine becoming a father.

Chapter Two

The Red Beanie

I never believed in love at first sight. Lust at first glance? Sure. Intrigue after an initial encounter? Definitely. But love, the most important thing of all? Absolutely not. And I most certainly didn't believe in it on the night of 28 April 2011.

I was at a gay bar nestled deep within the bustling streets of Hell's Kitchen, New York City. I'd come to Manhattan for four short days to visit my old roommate, Kristopher. I was a month away from graduating from college and finally fulfilling my childhood dream of moving to the Big Apple.

I desperately missed Kris, who had graduated a year ahead of me, so we'd decided to celebrate my twenty-third birthday together in the city. I also planned to audition for two Broadway musicals – you know, just to get a head start on my predestined path to stardom. And I wanted to see what was soon to be my new neighbourhood. I was anxious on the very best of days, so the thought of moving to New York was becoming quite overwhelming as I wrapped up my studies. It was daunting to exchange a small-town life for one in the concrete jungle. Dipping my toes into the dirty city water before plunging in headfirst a week after graduation seemed like a sensible plan.

Kris had graduated on time with a degree in Musical Theatre. I not-so-shockingly had become worried about my chances of making it big on Broadway and decided to stay at college for a fifth year in order to complete a second degree in Communications. This was a Plan B that, much like the morning-after pill, I hoped I would never have to use.

I was insanely jealous of Kris' New York escapades. We'd been attached at the hip for four years, so I met each Facebook post of his shenanigans in the city with equal parts jealousy and anger. But I was happy for him, too. By the time I visited, he'd found a great group of friends while scouting out the best bars and restaurants.

Kris' favourite drinking spot was a seedy two-storey mini club ironically called The Ritz. He wanted to introduce me to his gaggle of gays, so we took a sensible two hundred dollars out from an ATM and arrived at the club nice and early, by New York standards: 10 pm on the dot. Having not experienced the nightlife of a big city before, I was dressed in my finest New Hampshire outfit: black jean shorts, white high-top Converse sneakers, a loose grey V-neck t-shirt fresh off the H&M rack, and a red beanie purchased for two dollars from a Goodwill store. The hat had a small hole in it, which I decided made it much more fashionable. 'Very 90s heroin chic,' I told Kris as we got dressed.

'Oh, absolutely,' he replied, even though I'm sure he disagreed.

The Ritz was located on West 46th Street, between 8th and 9th Avenue. To my inexperienced New Hampshire eyes, it was the largest nightclub in the entire western hemisphere. Forget Disneyland: this was where dreams were made. Drag queens lip-synced in elaborate costumes atop glitter-covered stages, collecting dollar bills from emaciated twinks to the beat of Top 40 pop songs. Intoxicated patrons screamed off-key Madonna and Beyoncé lyrics for the entire city to hear.

An old man, maybe in his seventies, offered to buy me a drink the very second I landed at the bar. Before I knew it, he was promising to fly me to France for an all-inclusive romantic getaway. I politely declined, coyly batting my eyes. I turned to Kris and shouted, 'I think I'm going to like this place,' over the blaring of Lady Gaga's 'Born This Way'.

'You want a Jack & Ginger?'

'Yes, perfect,' I yelled back, with a massive smile on my face.

Soon I was drinking and dancing with Kris and his gorgeous group of friends. I wanted to avoid breaking the seal all night, but my fourth Jack & Ginger had other plans. I walked up the tiny stairs to the restroom, shoving my way past sweaty, glitter-covered men to join a long line. As I stood there, surrounded by more queer men than I had ever seen, I felt strangely at home. I had been to gay bars before, but they were much smaller. For the first time in my adult life, I was surrounded by hundreds of people who thought and danced and fucked like me. People who, I imagined, had also struggled with their sexuality and coming out to their parents. Some of them were probably from small towns and religious families like mine. Some had barely survived childhood before they'd rushed off to the accepting embrace of the city. Like them, in New York I was no longer alone.

I looked good and I felt good, the buzz of my fourth cocktail really kicking in. I was standing on the precipice of something magical, my entire adult life ahead of me. New Hampshire was my past, and New York was my future. Nothing could bring me down.

Then he appeared. He was walking past me when I caught his eye. I smiled at him, as one often does in the presence of someone physically attractive. He paused and glanced up at my floppy red beanie. 'Santa Claus called. He wants his hat back.' Was that a British accent? With a wink, the man strode into the gay abyss.

Stunned, but wanting desperately to seem unfazed, I shouted, 'Fuck you!' at the back of his purple polo shirt. He didn't turn to acknowledge my brilliant rebuttal, so I faced towards the restroom again and slipped the beanie into my right back pocket.

After returning to the bar, I drank a few more cocktails and danced to a dozen more songs with Kris and his friends. I couldn't help hoping to run into that strange British man again – in fact, I looked for him every chance I got, inserting turns into my dance routines to scan the room for his bushy eyebrows. But I couldn't find him.

I'd always been a bit of a masochist, loving a challenge. Whenever a guy at a club showed little interest in me, I made it my mission to win him over. And if he insulted me, either as a joke or out of spite, I refused to leave until he bought me a drink.

Who was that asshole? I thought as I made my way upstairs to find my spot in the bathroom line once more, the scene of the crime. *And when can he make fun of me again?*

Just like that, he appeared with a cocktail in his hand. 'You're not from around here, are you?' he shouted over Beyoncé's 'Single Ladies (Put a Ring on It)' in an accent that possibly wasn't British.

'That makes two of us,' I said. 'Nice shirt.'

'Really?' he asked, eyes wide.

'No,' I said, finally placing the accent. 'We stopped wearing polo shirts in America back in 2009. I'm so sorry, the memo must not have made it down under.'

He laughed and took a slow sip of his drink while staring directly into my soul.

It was then that I noticed his piercing blue eyes. I desperately wanted to retain his gaze, and I wasn't sure what was coming – I braced myself for a cocktail to the face or an insult so strong I'd be forced to walk out of the club with my tail between my legs.

'Ah, you're one of *those* gays,' he said. 'The "funny" ones.'

Like freshly poured cement, we sunk against the wall with no intention of retreating. I found out that his name was Josh Szeps. He was, in fact, Australian, born and raised in Sydney. He had an older brother named Amos, and a mother and father who were still married. He had been calling Manhattan home for the past six years, moving over on an Extraordinary Talent Visa to make it big in broadcasting. He had his own TV show on the Discovery Channel, didn't smoke cigarettes, and lived in the East Village with two roommates, both of whom were in the bar somewhere. Josh was only there because his straight female roommate had asked him to accompany her.

He was older than most of the boys I had dated, with salt-and-pepper stubble and designer jeans you could only afford if you were in your thirties or your seventies – which, to me, were almost the same thing.

I had never met anyone like him before. His accent was invigorating, his smile left me speechless, and his sense of humour – dry, sarcastic and perfectly timed like that of a professional stand-up comedian – left me with a permanent grin. I wasn't sure of much back then, and everything about New York was new and confusing, but I knew our chemistry was once-in-a-lifetime. From the moment we began speaking, there wasn't a single lull in our conversation.

'So what gave it away?' I asked, while he ordered us more drinks. 'What told you that I'm not from New York?'

'Honestly?' He leaned in close, like Mr Big from *Sex and the City*, grinning as he shouted into my ear over the loud music. 'You took your hat off. If you're a New Yorker and someone criticises you, you never roll over.' He pulled back, looked me in the eye and said, 'Go on, put it back on.'

I yanked the hat from my back pocket and tugged it onto my head. I'd be lying if I said I wasn't nervous. 'Good?' I sheepishly replied, hoping he saw an attractive young man worth pursuing and not Santa Claus' twink son.

'Nah … it's perfect.'

I smiled and prepared to offer up a 'thank you', but before I could he had cupped the side of my face and softly kissed me. It was flawlessly timed and somehow choreographed to match my exact kissing style. I hoped it would never end. In many ways, it never did.

★

Kris and I woke up early the next day, with massive hangovers that we quickly cured with a shared joint, Chinese takeaway, and a morning-long marathon of the best *American Idol* performances we could find on YouTube.

'Of course you met a man on your first night in New York City,' Kris said. 'You don't even live here yet and you're already sending out wedding invitations.'

'Stop it. I don't even know the guy.'

'You said "love" last night in the taxi.'

'I had forty-two cocktails last night, Kristopher. I could barely spell my last name. I can't be held accountable for anything I said.'

But the truth is, I did remember telling the Russian taxi driver that Josh was 'the type of guy you could fall in love with'. And I'd meant it.

Sure, meeting Josh in a dirty gay bar wasn't ideal – I'd have to leave that part out when I wrote a book about our whirlwind romance. But we had the 'it factor', that instant connection that everyone dreams of having. It was effortless, every second of it, as if we'd spent our lives preparing for that first encounter. I'd been giddy while it happened, and as I sat there taking a drag of the soggy joint the next day, I was still giddy. Like a schoolgirl, I was waiting by the phone for his call, certain that I had met the Australian man of my American dreams.

His ears must have been burning, because an hour later my butt began to vibrate.

G'day, mate! his text read.

No hablo española, I replied.

Solo muy poco, landed only a few seconds later. He was quick-witted.

Wait, you speak Spanish?

No. But I have this new website called Google.

Huh, never heard of it. Spanish porn?

Yeah, basically. Speaking of porn … are you free for lunch today?

I just cleared my schedule. What did you have in mind?

Balls, he texted back. *The meaty kind.*

A few hours later I met Josh at the Meatball Shop on the Lower East Side, leaving Kris to head off on a date of his own. Our lunch turned into drinks at the pub next door. Before I knew it, drinks turned into dinner and dinner into a late-night bar crawl around the city with his friends James and Julian.

At some point during the bar crawl, Josh and I agreed our connection was worth exploring further. I was going back to college in two days, but when I moved to New York City the following month we would meet up again and give it a real shot. I begged him to take me home that night, wanting nothing more than to seal the deal, but he had other plans. 'This is too special – let's not fuck it up.'

Two days later when I rocked up to the bus station to travel back to New Hampshire, I was shocked to see Josh standing there with a takeaway coffee in each hand. I hadn't told him when or how I was leaving; he had looked up the bus schedules and figured it out.

There he stood, my Australian, in an orange-and-purple striped polo shirt and a pair of torn acid-washed jeans. 'I couldn't wait an entire month to see you again.'

My heart was officially his.

He handed me my coffee, kissed me in front of the long line of passengers, helped me load my luggage onto the bus, and waved from the roadside as it pulled away.

I had thirty more days of college left, which I planned on enjoying with my friends. I would then rush back to New York City and seduce my Australian.

Josh and I spoke every day for two weeks. He was amazing at texting. The chemistry that we had in person translated perfectly in written form, so the foundation of our relationship was laid over that fortnight. I told every friend who would listen that I had met the man of my dreams, and I really believed it.

Then, unexpectedly, my Australian stopped responding to my messages: not for a day, or even a week, but for nine excruciating days. And because those nine days just so happened to be my final days of college, I buried my sadness in UFO Raspberries – my favourite beer at the time – and decided it simply wasn't meant to be. Hell, I was moving to New York City, where I had found an almost-boyfriend in less than twenty-four hours, so I was sure I could find another Australian man – or maybe a Brit – to call my own in no time.

Three days before I was due in New York, I received a text from Josh. He had 'lost his phone' on a 'train in Germany' while 'attending his brother's wedding'. I wasn't sure if I could or should believe him, but when he asked if I was available in three days' time to go on our second date, I said yes.

Do you have a tuxedo? he asked unexpectedly.

Of course I do, I lied.

And as quickly as I had decided the relationship wasn't meant to be, I forced my mother into the car with me and drove off to purchase some new formal wear.

Then, on 1 June, my parents and I left their home at 8 am and drove to New York City. We began moving my stuff into my apartment in Sunnyside, Queens, at 12 pm. We finished unpacking and said our teary goodbyes at 2 pm. I organised my room until around 4 pm, napped till 5 pm, showered at 5.15 pm, got dressed at 5.30 pm and left my apartment at 6 pm to meet Josh at the top of the Lincoln Center steps for our second date.

On my first night living in New York, I sat in the audience of a World Science Festival Gala, well and truly in the process of falling in love with my Australian.

★

While our first few meetings felt like they had been ripped from the pages of a gay fairytale, the initial chapters of our love story were far from perfect. Some couples experience a 'Honeymoon Phase' where it seems like nothing could go wrong, but Josh and I waded through months of what I referred to as the 'Uncertainty Stage'. We had so much in common and were very attracted to each other, but the realities of our ten-year age gap and cultural differences were hard to navigate, alongside the major life changes I was grappling with.

As soon as Josh began to introduce me to his friends, I got the sense they didn't take me seriously. I received a constant stream of 'you're so adorable', which left me feeling inadequate at a stage of our relationship where I wanted to feel like an equal. On top of that, Josh had quickly become my tour guide in the Big Apple. Whenever I had a problem with navigating transportation or a basic question about where to find Cuban food, I would just text the number labelled 'My Australian' in my phone contacts. Without knowing it, we had established a teacher–student dynamic that neither of us really wanted.

It didn't help that I had never had a big kid job before and was making the difficult decision to leave performing behind in order to pursue a more stable career in a brand-new industry called 'social media'. My anxiety was extreme, so Josh witnessed me becoming distant and detached – and randomly leaving his apartment in the middle of the night out of pure embarrassment. Because I was so adept at hiding my panic attacks and breakdowns, he assumed I was just a cold, withdrawn asshole at times.

Then there were the cultural differences, even though Josh had lived in America for six years. There were obvious things like the metric system, colloquialisms, and national approaches to healthcare, gun laws and even tipping culture. But then there were much more complex things, wired into the core of our personalities, which soon caused friction. Aussies, I learned, have 'tall poppy syndrome', whereas Americans, on average, praise showmanship and standing out in a crowd. Americans pride ourselves on how much we attend to our careers, while Aussies value a stronger work–life balance. In general, while Aussies consider months-long international travel to be a rite of passage and form of self-care, Americans consider ten days off to be a generous holiday. And I wasn't most Americans: I was much worse. I was obsessed with getting ahead and thought it was a badge of honour not to take time off. The more days I had left at the end of the year, the more likely I was to be promoted. When Josh booked us an overseas holiday not long after we met, I refused to go and told him I couldn't leave my job for that long. He cancelled the trip, baffled.

To make matters worse, Josh and I totally disagreed about having children.

'I love kids!' I said while watching a mom attempt to wrangle her screaming toddler on the street.

'Do you want kids?' Josh asked.

'Oh, no. Absolutely not. Let's leave that challenge to the straights.'

'Really? I always imagined I'd have kids one day.'

'Then find yourself another man,' I replied, with equal parts wit and honesty (or lack thereof).

'But don't you think you'll feel that you missed out on something when you're older?'

'I'll be fine,' I said. 'I'll wipe away the tears with my hard-earned cash that I get to spend on myself.'

It was hard to navigate the tangled web of our differences. Two months into dating Josh, I wrote in my diary:

*I'm not sure if this relationship is going to last. I'm just not sure
if it's possible to date someone from another country. It's fun
in theory, sexy even, but difficult to navigate when you don't
share a mutual script. I understand why so many people end up
marrying someone from their town or state. There's less hurdles
to jump over and right now I feel like our entire relationship is a
series of pole vaults over major differences.*

But four days later, everything changed. I had been working the dinner shift at a popular Italian restaurant in SoHo. I worked five days a week, with Tuesday and Wednesday nights off. On work nights the restaurant would close at 11 pm, and I'd roll out the door an hour later if everything went according to plan. Most nights, I'd take the 7 train home and pass out after midnight, halfway through an episode of *Sex and the City*. But on most Friday and Saturday nights, Josh would meet me at the restaurant. He'd grab a drink with my boss, and then we'd get lost in the NYC nightlife, which would just be picking up steam.

There's something you need to understand about Josh: at his core, he is a philosopher. He passed the Mensa test but didn't want to join the club. I was a simple boy from a small-ish town; a hard worker who got good grades but never considered himself a real thinker. My spare time was spent analysing *America's Next Top Model*, not pondering the meaning of life. Josh pushed me to develop a critical-thinking muscle, empowering me to form judgements on complex issues. This is one of the main reasons I fell in love with him: his approach to existence sat so far outside my comfort zone that it felt like he was handing me a new lease on life. He helped me come to believe that my perception of the world is as valid as that of a Harvard Law professor. The more I critically analysed, the more holes I found, and the more holes I found, the more determined I felt to try and change them – even just in my own tiny circles in New York City and back in New Hampshire.

One Saturday night, Josh and I stumbled upon a martini bar in the East Village shortly after he picked me up from work. The bar, strangely, was almost empty. When we pushed through a velvet curtain at the back, we found ourselves in a sea of pillows, couches and plush chairs. We picked a romantic spot by a fireplace in the dimly lit room.

'I had a thought,' Josh said, after coming back from the bar with our drinks. 'What would it look like if people approached their relationships like they were never going to end?'

Sure that he was being cheeky, I said, 'If this is a proposal, I will require a prenup.'

Josh laughed, kissed me passionately over our matching cocktails, and dove straight into a relationship pitch. 'Bad relationships need to end, don't get me wrong. But I reckon as a society, we've found ourselves in a break-up pandemic. Our parents' generation and the generations before that worked harder to keep their relationships alive.'

'They didn't really have another option, did they?' I pushed back. 'Divorce wasn't acceptable, not back then. Women were forced to stay in unhealthy relationships, and men just fucked around. Maybe the break-up pandemic is in response to that?'

As our discussion continued, Josh and I began to unpick our past relationships. We found themes in successful marriages we'd seen growing up, reflected on communication strategies that had worked with our exes, and fantasised about a relationship in which we actively worked to stay together. At that martini bar, we challenged each other to take a 'till death do us part' approach to our partnership. Long before we even discussed moving in together, we agreed to treat our relationship as seriously as a married couple might. If there was a problem, even a tiny one, we'd talk about it. If things weren't working, we'd exhaust all options. If we had an issue, we'd go to couples counselling. Instead of waiting for a proposal, we'd begin today.

That night changed the trajectory of my life. From that moment forward, we met every difference we had – even the smallest disagreement – as a challenge. Instead of thinking of our relationship as disposable, we encouraged each other to do the work. We learned, with time, to take each other's concerns seriously, always keeping a long-term future in mind.

I would ask myself, *If I really want this relationship to last, how should I approach this tiny issue in the present? Should I bottle up the frustration or have the conversation now? If we get married and have two children and move to Australia one day, will I be proud of how I tackled this seemingly insignificant hurdle today?*

★

We moved in together after just eleven months. We found a tiny apartment in Brooklyn Heights, just one subway stop out of Manhattan, on Pineapple Street. We liked the idea of being the fruitiest occupants on such a fruity-ass lane, and we absolutely were. In that tiny apartment with a borderline illegal kitchenette and a cramped hallway closet, we started our not-so-tiny life together.

I met Josh's parents, Mary Ann and Henri, at a local diner. I instantly delighted in their relaxed Aussie spirit and their passion for dissecting the world's biggest issues; the brilliant, interesting and passionate apple hadn't fallen far from the tree. Josh met my parents, in true American fashion, at an IHOP. He delighted in their humour and charm, remarking on their youthful energy along with the special love they had for each other and me.

Before I knew it, Josh's friends were mine and mine became his. He would go to Kris' bar, Flaming Saddles, to grab drinks without me. I started working for his friend James as a way to get marketing experience before applying for agency jobs. Josh once spent the day at an amusement park with Joe because I hated roller-coasters.

Josh and I were now an 'us'. Thai food was *our* food, jazz music was *our* music, *Anthony Bourdain: No Reservations* was *our* television show. Christmas cards were addressed to *Sean & Josh*, and wedding invitations had our names next to one another in gold calligraphy. We even started calling each other 'monkey', *our* own endearing nickname.

I don't know exactly when it happened, but somewhere along the way I began to see a future where I could get married. In fact, now it was the only thing I wanted. Him, Josh, my Australian – I wanted him to be my husband.

Two years, seven months and seven days after I met Josh at The Ritz in Hell's Kitchen, we were on vacation in Koh Samui, Thailand. Josh had somehow persuaded me to take two weeks off. We found ourselves relaxing in a luxury villa, overlooking the Gulf of Thailand from a secluded hill on Koh Samui's south-western tip.

An issue with our room had caused Josh to argue with the staff upon arrival. I would later learn that it was all staged, but at the time I felt total discomfort as the French hospitality worker apologised profusely and offered us dinner in the Presidential Villa.

There were roses and blazing candles on our table, which had been set with a pair of stainless-steel cloches. Two Thai waiters stood beside us, each with one hand placed behind his back. After they helped us into our seats, the first cloche was lifted. Inside was a handwritten note: *Have I told you today that you're my favourite person in the world?*

I looked up at Josh and smiled. He had been asking me that question for at least a year, every morning before work. I always replied with, 'Nope', and he'd say, 'Oops. You're my favourite person in the world.'

So when one of the waiters lifted up the second cloche to reveal a cream cake with *Oops* iced onto it, I was excited but not surprised. I said, 'Thank you', with a cheeky grin as Josh stood up to walk my way. The truth didn't cross my mind – not for a second. I thought he was coming over to give me a kiss.

He dropped to one knee, pulled out a red velvet ring box, and said, 'You're my favourite person in the world. Will you marry me?'

I said 'yes', of course – but only after thirty minutes of crying so aggressively that the waiters had to awkwardly back out of the room and go hide. 'I've never been better,' I told my fiancé. And I wasn't lying.

I've never believed in love at first sight. What I do believe in, especially after twelve years in a relationship with the love of my life, my Australian, is that you can – with the snap of your fingers – choose to take a relationship seriously. You can meet someone, be blown away by the potential of your relationship, and then choose to treat it like there's no way out. And sure, that relationship might end. The effort you put in might not be reciprocated. But maybe, just maybe, you'll meet a person who is committed to making it work with you.

You'll fall in love and move in together after eleven months. He'll propose to you in Thailand two years later. You'll get married – first in a surprise wedding on the steps where you met for your second date, then again at your grandmother's house in New Hampshire, surrounded by your closest friends and family, including your mother and father, your brother and sister, Mary Ann and Henri, Amos, Kristopher, Joe and James. And finally you'll have a third wedding celebration, a 1920s-style party at the Ensemble Theatre in Sydney, Australia.

Then maybe, if you're really lucky, you'll decide to start a family together.

Josh and me in my abuela's backyard for our New Hampshire wedding celebration.

Chapter Three

The C-Word

I've always been more of a glass-half-empty kind of guy. I could try and blame my mother for this, because she tends to prepare for worst-case scenarios, but it's really just my anxious brain – wired during childhood, and fed on fear of God and homophobia. My slightly pessimistic worldview has left me with an ever-present distrust of people. Or maybe 'distrust' is the wrong word: it's left me with an ever-present suspicion that hovers above most people's heads as I come in contact with them.

The biggest issue about having a brain like this is that my anxiety is reinforced by all the negativity being pumped into my veins via media and gossip. The second my glass is filled with positivity, another article pops up in my timeline to remind me just how terrible humans can be – another shooting, another affair, another queerphobic attack, another crooked politician working double time to tear down his opponent with an exaggerated claim, which half the population will feed on like a pack of wolves.

The C-Word

This was the pattern I followed for most of my young life. People are good, people are bad, people are good, people are bad. That is, until we started the surrogacy journey.

★

When I first met Josh, he wanted kids and I did not. But slowly, during our time together in New York City, things started to shift. Unbeknown to both of us, while we were falling in love and building a life together, we began trying on each other's perspectives on parenthood. Josh thought that being with me meant he wouldn't have kids. Over drinks one night, he claimed that he 'could be happy with just the two of us'. But during that same period, as the world became more accepting of queer people, I began to see my disdain for parenthood for what it truly was: internalised homophobia masked as a personality trait.

We lived in one of the gayest, most diverse and accepting places on the planet. As the years flew by, I started to notice more and more gay parents as I walked the streets of Brooklyn. Each time I saw an adorable queer family, I'd question my stance on becoming a gay dad. The pressure of being the lonely outcast in a sea of straightness, which might have been the case had I stayed in New Hampshire, was no longer an issue. In fact, I would easily have found a network of gay dads in my local area.

'We'd be really good at that,' I said to Josh one night after leaving his friend Denis' apartment. We'd just had dinner with Denis and his husband, who were fostering a child.

Josh smirked. 'I thought you didn't want to have kids?'

'I also thought I was going to marry a Backstreet Boy, monkey.' I laughed. 'I can't be held accountable for the things I've said in the past.'

'But I agree. We'd be great dads. Have you changed your mind?'

'I think I have.'

Then, shortly after our wedding in New Hampshire – and by 'shortly' I mean two days – I dropped the c-word over brunch.

'How soon after getting married is too soon to have children?' I asked Josh.

'According to Alabama Law, you're supposed to get pregnant before marriage and then hitched a few days before you pop,' he joked.

'But, for real. How soon?'

'The process could take years, so we could start right now,' he suggested.

And that's exactly what we did.

At first we thought adoption and fostering were our only options, because Josh had a moral aversion to the growing trend of surrogacy in poorer countries. He didn't believe in 'renting the womb' of a person who was only doing it for the money. We researched the best adoption agencies in New York and signed up for their introductory sessions, but the message we took away was that the process was interminable and there were no guarantees.

I stumbled upon a Facebook post that set a new course for us. A college friend of mine, Lynden, posted that she was pregnant again. I saw the picture before reading the caption, which explained that, while she was in fact pregnant, the child wasn't hers: she was a surrogate. She had two kids of her own, and she'd chosen to carry a child for a gay man. The embryo had been created from the egg of a donor paired with the man's sperm. Lynden was selflessly helping this man start his family. While she was receiving some compensation, she didn't need the money – she was doing this out of the goodness of her heart.

My mind was, quite literally, blown. Before messaging Lynden for more details, I raced to Google. I'd heard that the actor Neil Patrick Harris had twins with his husband, but until then I'd had no idea how that had happened. I knew instantly, after reading just one article, that this was the path I wanted to take. I could feel it in my bones. The idea of using our own sperm and finding an egg donor who looked like one of us, or even shared our cultural makeup, was very alluring. I discovered that family members across the globe were donating their eggs or sperm to their gay sons, siblings or cousins, allowing them to have a child that was genetically related. I felt an instant connection to that option. I remember thinking that it was my chance to be as close to normal as I'd ever get. After a lifetime of thinking that it would be impossible to find a man and produce a child that was genetically ours, it seemed that it was possible. That I had a chance to make my childhood fantasies a reality.

Luckily, Josh felt the same. As long as there was no power imbalance with the surrogate and she was choosing this with complete freedom, my husband and I were in. We just needed to make the money work – it would cost hundreds of thousands of dollars – and find an agency to assist us. We cancelled the remaining adoption sessions and redirected our search efforts: we were going to find both an egg donor and a surrogate.

★

At the beginning of the surrogacy process, I often found myself second-guessing our plan. A very close friend, a fellow gay man, told me within seconds of hearing the news that I was 'just trying to be like the straights' when I'd been given a 'Get Out of Parenting-Jail Free Card'. Another gay friend asked me, 'How could you choose surrogacy when so many children need to be adopted?' Their words felt like heavy baggage that I had to drag from appointment to appointment. But I knew their own internalised homophobia was at play – that and a toxic potion of judgement, jealousy and ignorance. After all, I could relate.

Josh and I were still a long way away from being fathers. We needed to find an agency, a surrogate, an egg donor, an IVF clinic and a lawyer. But making those important decisions would be insanely difficult with a glass–half-empty mentality. There were many hurdles to jump over, and I had to believe that we were capable of leaping and landing again if we were ever going to make it to the finish line. But instead of being excited about the prospect of finding an egg donor, I was drowning in a sea of anxious thoughts. *What if I can't find a woman who looks like me? What if I make the wrong decision and accidentally give my children terrible genes? What if my kids get in touch with their mom one day and they're disappointed with what they find? What if I'm disappointed?* This 'what if' mindset affected every part of the surrogacy process. *How can we possibly know if we're making the right decision about a surrogate? Are we educated enough to decide which fertility specialist is the best? Have we picked the right agency? Are we ruining these poor children's lives?*

I felt as though my true self – the happy man who had decided to have children with the love of his life – was fading away. I was so frustrated, consumed by an endless stream of emails and reviews and negative thoughts, that I wondered if I was even capable of being a dad at all. *If people are inherently bad*, I thought, *and the process is shit, and my friends don't trust my decision, and there's no obvious answer to any one choice that must be made in a timely fashion, then maybe I'm just not cut out for fatherhood?*

Normal people, I wrote down during a therapy session in New York City, *wouldn't react this way. People who are ready to be parents don't struggle like this.*

And then, right on cue, two women gave me the emotional lifebuoy I so desperately needed, not just to survive the surrogacy journey but also to thrive.

On New Year's Day 2016, Josh and I caught the Eurostar train from London to Paris for a holiday. That night in our hotel room, I FaceTimed with various family members to wish them a happy new year. Josh and I were speaking to one of the women in my family, exchanging chitchat and learning about her weekend plans, when her expression turned serious. 'There's something I have to tell you two,' she said. 'I've been thinking about it a lot over the past year, and I've decided to give you my eggs.'

My world stopped. The sounds of Paris disappeared, the ambient noise from her holiday party drifted away, and I was left with the pounding of my heart. I gasped, covered my mouth and looked at Josh as tears began to pool for us both. I handed the phone over to him before I fell back onto the bed. The happiest and warmest emotions poured out of me as I cried.

Had this really just happened? Had I actually understood her words? Up until that moment, I'd been under the impression that, while many of my friends and family members had listened to my lectures about egg donation, none of them would be willing to make such a selfless offer. I wouldn't have blamed them – of course not. I'm not sure if I would have been strong enough to hand over such a personal gift.

This was a momentous, life-altering decision with ramifications around every corner. She had to be prepared for invasive surgery. For the potential of experiencing complications that could, in very rare cases, make it difficult for her to have biological children in the future. For the potential that my children would one day see her as their mother. For the potential of enduring unexpected emotional trauma from coming into contact with them periodically for the rest of her adult life. For the potential, god forbid, that our relationship would somehow be ruined by the experience and that our extended family would be torn apart.

It wasn't easy for her, not in the slightest. In fact, it was possibly the hardest decision she'd ever have to make. But she told us firmly that after months of research and careful consideration, multiple conversations and a few therapy sessions, she had made her choice.

I sat up from the bed to thank her, wiping away my tears. Finally, after all I'd been through, my dream of being a father to children who were not just biologically mine but also my husband's was within reach. Because of this woman, this selfless goddess, I was being given a rare opportunity, one of the first hundreds of its kind in human history.

A scene popped into my head of a young child, my child, rushing in from primary school while waving a piece of paper. 'Dada,' they shouted. 'I have to fill out this family tree for school. Can you help me?'

'Of course I can,' I replied, without skipping a beat. 'Pull up a chair and let's fill it in together.'

★

The second woman was a complete stranger.

As soon as the gift of egg donation was handed to us, we pushed forward through the surrogacy process with a new-found sense of determination. I sent an email requesting information from Circle Surrogacy, a full-service agency that provided support to both intended parents – as in, people who can't conceive on their own – and surrogates. My mother-in-law, Mary Ann, had told us about the company, which had glowing reviews and a high success rate. When Josh and I returned from Europe, I set up an initial information session for 14 January 2016. After that, we went back and forth by email, requesting more details about the cost and the legal rights of intended parents, and by late January we were satisfied with their responses. We sorted out our finances during February and March. Then, on 30 March, we finally pulled the trigger: we officially signed with Circle Surrogacy.

One of the reasons we decided to go with Circle was their unique method of pairing intended parents with surrogates. We'd encountered several other agencies that used what Josh and I referred to as a 'folder selection' process, where you simply pick up a folder packed full of previously approved surrogates, then flip from woman to woman until you find one who meets your criteria. Honestly, this method didn't sit well with us. Sure, we were hacking a system and paying a surrogate to carry our child, but did it need to feel like we were choosing a dinner table from a catalogue? These were real women, potential friends, potential family members, not items to be ranked against each other and purchased based off a photo and a few sentences.

Circle believed in matching one surrogate with one family. We would still have the legally required background checks, the psychological assessments, the pre-interviews and the in-home inspections, but instead of giving intended parents a folder of options, Circle would narrow them down to one perfect pairing. After two decades in the business, they believed they could find exactly what intended parents were looking for based on a long list of details that we provided.

One day, weeks after completing our paperwork and interviews, we received an email: a short description, a few family photos, and a series of attachments that outlined the results of our surrogate's initial interviews. Part of the email read: *Sara is a 31-year-old married mother of 3 children living in Wisconsin. She maintains a career as a registered nurse.* We immediately devoured the paperwork but kept coming back to the family photos – the smiles on her children's faces, the warm embrace from her husband.

The following morning at 6.02, Josh emailed back with, *We LOVE her.* At 12.03 pm we received an email from Circle that read, *I heard from the carrier and she is available to Skype with you tonight at 8:30 PM CST.* It was happening.

For the first time in the process, I felt giddy with nervous excitement, like I was about to go in for an important job interview. *I hope she likes us*, I messaged Kris.

Let's hope you love her as much as I'm sure she's going to love you, he replied.

That night after dinner, Josh and I snuggled onto our purple couch in our brownstone apartment in Park Slope, Brooklyn, and waited patiently for the video chat to connect. In front of us sat Sara, a beautiful brunette with short, straight hair and a smile that stretched from ear to ear. Beside her sat a teddy bear of a human named Nate. They both radiated joy and a sense of calm.

'I'm so nervous,' I blurted out to break the ice.

'Me too,' Sara replied. 'I've been nervous all day.'

During that thirty-minute call, we learned a little more about one another, and Josh and I fell in love with their Minnesota accents.

'Why do you want to be a surrogate?' Josh asked.

'I just really love being pregnant.' Sara laughed, putting us all at ease. 'When we decided we were done having kids, I was really sad that I wouldn't get to experience it all again.'

'Did you know about surrogacy because of your work?' I asked.

'A colleague of mine was carrying a child, and I congratulated her. I found out it was actually for another family, so that's how I learned about it.'

Nate joined in. 'She came home and told me about it, and we've been talking about it ever since.'

A few minutes later, I asked an important question; one that had been on my mind since the beginning of this process. 'Obviously, we're gay. I saw in your paperwork that it isn't an issue for you, but how do you think your family will feel about all of this?'

'My family is very accepting. They find this unusual, obviously. My dad thought it was very strange at first, the whole surrogacy thing, but they've come around. And when we were filling out the forms and deciding what types of families we might want to help, I thought what a great gift it would be to carry for a gay couple – a couple who really needs us. The other thing is that where we're from, there just isn't a lot of diversity, and we think this would be such a great way to teach our three children about the world.'

When those words fell from her mouth, I knew for sure that she was the one.

'We'd love to introduce you to our kids,' Sara added. 'Ideally we'd keep them involved in the process, both throughout the pregnancy and after the birth.'

As soon as we ended the call, I started crying into Josh's shoulder. He instantly agreed that not only was Sara the perfect surrogate, but that she and Nate and their loving family were the exact humans we had been hoping for.

Josh and I had secretly been fantasising about finding a surrogate who would quickly become a member of the family. We'd travel to see each other, spend holidays together, exchange Christmas cards, and encourage our children to treat them like extended family. Not only did this idea warm our hearts, but we thought it would be helpful too. We knew that having two dads and no mom might be challenging for our kids, so maintaining a close relationship with our surrogate seemed like a smart way to eliminate any potential confusion and feelings of not knowing the truth about where they came from.

My top priority was to make it clear to my children, however many we had, that they were surrounded by love every step of the way. Even though they didn't have a mother, they had a tribe of adults committed to them and their well-being.

Within minutes of that video chat, Josh and I called Circle and let them know we were happy to proceed. Sara and Nate did the exact same thing, so the next morning we received the following email from the agency: *Hi Sara, Josh and Sean, I wanted to say congratulations to all of you, you are now officially matched!*

★

The surrogacy process was emotionally and financially draining. We spent more than A$240,000 while existing in a constant state of disconnect from the medical realities. Sara lived in Minnesota and later Wisconsin; we lived in New York City and then moved to Los Angeles; our egg donor was from the Northeast. Josh and I found it hard to feel invested in the experience of becoming parents while being so physically distanced.

After our egg donor experienced a minor complication post-retrieval and passed out on the flight home, she was in bed for forty-eight hours in pain. Josh and I were across the country in Los Angeles, and we both had demanding jobs, so we were only able to assist with phone calls and a series of 'we're sorry' and 'thank you' messages. She made a full recovery and totally understood why we couldn't be there, but it still hurt all of us. Most couples edge towards parenthood over nine increasingly arduous months for the pregnant partner, whereas we sometimes forgot we were even 'pregnant'.

One night a few months into our pregnancy, we were watching TV, getting a little high and eating our favourite Thai takeaway. It was the season finale of *Top Chef: Charleston*. During a commercial break, we began poking fun at all the contestants who used parenthood as their emotional hook during confessionals. We giggled at how silly it seemed that they were apparently 'doing it for my kid' and not for themselves.

'Parents are so stupid,' I said to Josh as he shoved some curry wrapped in roti into his mouth.

He tried talking, then indicated with a finger that I should wait. After swallowing his food, he took a sip of water and said, 'We're parents, Sean. We're pregnant right now.'

I had completely forgotten. With no swelling belly in our house as a constant reminder of what was to come, plus the help of a THC haze, I had forgotten for a moment that we were, in fact, about to be dads. I could drink red wine, and our surrogate couldn't. I could get high, and our surrogate wouldn't. I could eat whatever spicy food I wanted to and then giggle about parenthood like it was someone else's issue. And that, we agreed, was very strange.

But in the end, we knew we were lucky. We had a once-in-a-lifetime gift from a donor who was related to me, and we were paired with a surrogate who wanted to remain a part of our family. Two amazing women were willing to put their physical health at risk so that we could become fathers. One of the greatest gifts I received through this process was the knowledge that selfless people really do exist. Now, thanks to those amazing women, instead of thinking about a glass being half full or half empty, I'm grateful to have a glass at all.

Chapter Four

The Sex Bomb

'Do you have a preference for the sex of your children?'

It wasn't a question I'd expected to be asked that morning. Actually, it wasn't a question I'd expected to be asked *ever*. I hadn't even known it was possible, let alone legal, to choose the sex of your children.

'During the genetic testing process, intended parents like yourselves can choose to learn the sex chromosomes of each viable embryo,' we were told by our IVF specialist, Doctor Vicken Sahakian from the Pacific Fertility Center of Los Angeles.

'That's some *Star Trek* shit,' I said under my breath to Josh, who was sitting beside me in our living room as we stared at the doctor on my laptop screen.

'Is this standard in America?' Josh asked. 'I didn't know this was allowed.'

'It's not legal in every country, including Australia,' Dr Sahakian replied. 'And it isn't compulsory here, but it's an option since you've decided to do genetic testing.'

'We'll go away and discuss it,' Josh chimed in. He was good like that, always knowing when to stall without jumping in and making rash decisions – unlike me: who preferred to answer straight away and then beg for forgiveness when the decision inevitably changed.

We hung up the Zoom call, and I looked at Josh. 'To choose, or not to choose.'

'That is the question,' he replied.

We'd decided earlier on that we would prefer to put in two embryos and had selected a surrogate willing to carry multiples. I grew up surrounded by twins, at school and in my extended family, so I felt comfortable at the thought of raising them. Josh, who loved children but was no fan of tiny babies, was drawn to what he called an 'instant family'. If both embryos survived, we'd avoid the financial and emotional hardship of repeating the entire process. Also, implanting two embryos increased the chance that one of them would survive by around fifty per cent; at least, that was the data back then.

We left the living room, which looked out onto a bustling Brooklyn street, and made our way into the quieter bedroom and bathroom. Josh brushed his teeth and prepared for a shower, while I lay in bed in our pitch-dark room. He spoke to me loudly over the flow of the faucet, sounding as if we were already in agreement. 'I reckon it's pretty straightforward.'

He didn't have a problem with keeping the process as 'normal' as possible. We could simply advise the doctor to use the most viable embryos, and we'd find out the sexes just like every other parent before us. But Josh also loved the idea of choosing one male and one female. That way, if only one embryo developed, we'd still learn about the sex in an exciting reveal; if both took, we'd have the rare gift of raising both sexes at the same time.

But I didn't 'reckon' it was straightforward at all. The thing was, I wasn't sold on having a daughter. In fact, I was adamantly against it. The thought made me just about as nervous as the idea of dating a woman.

'We should have two boys,' I shouted over the sound of running water.

Josh turned off the faucet and poked his head out into the bedroom, a shocked look on his face. 'Why not a girl?'

'Because men shouldn't raise daughters by themselves,' I said with certainty.

'You're joking.' He stared at me, now with a much more concerned expression.

'I'm not.' I sat up on the edge of our bed and locked eyes with him. 'We're not women, Josh. How the hell are we supposed to support a daughter through all the challenges she's going to face?'

'The same way single parents support children – or, I don't know, straight couples who support gay kids.'

'This feels different. We haven't had periods or grown breasts. Do you even know how to put in a tampon or braid long hair?'

'We'll figure it all out. We'll ask our mums. We'll learn as we go.'

'She's going to want a mom, Josh. She just will. And I won't be able to handle that heartbreak. It's already hard enough for me to feel like we're giving them a more difficult life. If we can eliminate challenges, we should. I don't think I'd be a good dad to a daughter.'

Shortly after this discussion, I called my mom and presented my case.

The tone of her voice told me that she couldn't believe we were allowed to make such a decision, but she managed to say, 'I know you'd be great fathers no matter the gender of the child. We might have leveraged our personal experience more or less with each of you, but gender very rarely came into play. I'd love for you to have experience with both sexes, like we did, but I know you'll make the decision that's right for you and Josh.'

'That's nice,' I replied. 'But not very helpful. Can't you just tell me what to do?'

*

Josh worked hard that week to present his case, but night after night we went to bed without an answer. Sadly we couldn't see eye to eye on this wildly important decision.

What it really came down to for me was that I was afraid.

It's important to note that at the time I had these fears, my understanding of gender, sex and sexuality was very limited. Although I knew that gender diverse people existed, I didn't think I knew any of them personally. But for most of my life, there weren't public discussions around being non-binary, like there are today, and I almost always thought of gender in terms of men and women, moms and dads, sons and daughters. Even as a gay person, I saw parenting problems as straight, cisgender problems.

Parenthood was this massive, scary mountain that I wanted desperately to climb and climb well. I knew that no one can truly be prepared for the rude realities of raising tiny humans, but I wanted to set myself and Josh up for success. The mother was the primary caregiver in the vast majority of families. Of course, I knew that single fathers and gay male couples raised daughters, but I was under the impression that those girls suffered. I thought motherless daughters grew up lacking the necessary lessons only a mom could provide. It wasn't like I was pulling this out of thin air – I didn't have to look far to see that the parenting space was mother-dominated. It seemed that every article, every book, and every television and radio segment was about the mom and her importance. Dads apparently weren't as capable, according to a media landscape that was failing me miserably.

When I dropped the sex-selection bomb on my friends and co-workers, nearly every woman admitted that if she had the choice she'd pick a girl. Meanwhile, the men all wanted sons. 'Dads almost always get more excited during male gender reveal parties, and it's the moms who cry hysterically when the stupid boxes contain pink balloons,' a colleague shared during our lunchbreak. 'Of course they love their kids, but there's something deeper going on here – a strange animal instinct to want to see ourselves in our children.'

I also looked to examples in my own life. My mother had taught my sister how to shave her legs and put in a tampon. She'd taken her to get her ears pierced and her hair done, and helped her pick out clothes for each school term. She'd taken her to cheerleading, while my father had taken my brother to American football practice. Whenever something had gone wrong in my sister's life, with boys or her friendship group, she had run straight to Mom. I believed our mother possessed an innate drive to pass down her female wisdom in all its intricacies, like her mother had done for her, and her abuela, my great-grandmother, before that. I was afraid of failing my daughter – I didn't want her to grow up without a strong female role model in the house; a woman who could predict her needs based on a lifetime of experience.

I kept trying to explain to Josh that I wasn't insane for thinking along these lines. He had to go on a trip to Australia, so we stalled in responding to our doctor but didn't stop talking to each other. Late at night for me and early in the morning for him, we continued our Battle of the Sexes.

'We want to be parents,' Josh said. 'That's it. We're not doing this to have a boy. We're not hedging our bets on an able-bodied straight child. We just want to be dads.'

'I know that … but don't you think you'd be better suited to being a father to a boy?'

'I don't. A male child will have upsides and downsides. A female child will have upsides and downsides. I want to experience it all. I want to be a daddy to a girl!'

I pushed back again. 'I don't think you're living in the real world.'

'If you know that you'd be a great father to a boy, then you have to believe you'd be just as great to a girl. We can't make decisions for a child we don't know yet. What if they come out as trans? Will you instantly go from being a great dad to a shit one?'

Though I wasn't willing to admit it to him on the phone, that's when it clicked. It was like a well-needed slap across my close-minded face.

I had developed an unfounded theory about parenting and until now had refused to consider that it might be misguided. I'd thought that as a man raising a boy, I would know how to deal with every tough question, every life stage and every developmental milestone, because they would be just like mine were − or similar enough. Somehow, I'd fallen into the trap that had caught generations of dads before me: men who expected their sons to follow in their footsteps. Then there were the generations of moms who assumed their husbands would deal with the 'manly' things while they tackled 'girly' activities with their daughters. This way of parenting failed children who didn't fit the mould. I should have known better.

I couldn't make decisions for my kids, because I didn't know them yet. Sure, my son might have questions about his penis that Josh and I would feel confident answering, but he might also want to learn about makeup or rugby or flying a plane, and we would have to do some research. My daughter might become obsessed with drag queens or want to star in a musical, and that would be my moment to shine.

I was going to love my kids and deliver the parenting goods no matter what. I wouldn't say 'no' just because our sex chromosomes and genitalia didn't match. I'd learn, I'd grow, and I'd stretch outside my comfort zone. Like my husband, I would walk into the experience with an open mind.

★

After a few days of nursing my wounded ego, I told Josh that he was right.

'The fact that we're having these types of conversations now puts us one step ahead of most parents,' he kindly offered, not one to gloat.

We emailed Dr Sahakian: *Sex isn't an issue for us. Ideally, we'd have one boy and one girl placed into the womb. Please just prioritise putting the most viable embryos in.*

A few months later, Sara and Nate flew to Los Angeles, where we all met face to face for the first time. During a routine IVF implantation, Josh and I sat on either side of Sara, holding her hands. On a screen above us, we watched Dr Sahakian place our two embryos on the inner layer of her uterus. Afterwards, Sara and Nate rested in a nearby hotel before flying home. We all waited patiently and were thrilled by a positive pregnancy test.

On 8 February 2017, after six weeks of gestation, Sara had her first real follow-up appointment with her local doctor, which Josh and I attended via FaceTime. Huddled in our LA apartment, we found out that both embryos had taken. We were having twins.

This is a photo of us with Sara, our gorgeous surrogate, moments after the embryo transfer in Los Angeles.

Chapter Five

The Itch

On a personality scale where the love of new experiences sits eagerly on one side and the fear of change sits anxiously on the other, you will find me balancing in the middle in an annoyingly perfect split. It's not that I like change – in fact, I have consistently demonstrated an inability to cope with it in the short term. It's just that something deep inside of me has always been drawn to the new. Some would say that this is a result of growing up in the digital generation, as though I'm an addict looking for his next dopamine hit. Others might say it's a coping mechanism to deal with unhappiness. But while I'm sure that my social media obsession and mental health history play their parts, I've always blamed my small-town upbringing for my obsession with novelty.

As a kid, I longed for something more. I always knew I was the black sheep in my small-ish town. I felt that all eyes were on me, and in a town where you can name the passengers of every car that passes you by, that might often have been true. When things got difficult, I'd fantasise about running away to places where I could get lost in the crowd and where nobody knew my name. And when everyone in town found out through the grapevine that I was gay, my playful relocation fantasies shifted in tone from dreamy to desperate. I wanted to be surrounded by people like me, or at least people who accepted people like me.

When I relocated to Sunnyside, Queens, I discovered that all the rumours about big cities were true. New York City was diverse, eclectic, fast-paced and very queer. You could walk the streets naked, pee on a subway platform during rush hour, or build a fort on the side of the road and invite all the local rats to move in with you, and no one would bat an eye. You could stand out as a proud gay man while blending in entirely and bothering not a single soul. The city was everything I'd desperately needed as a gay child, and it was just a few hours' drive from my childhood home. By moving there, I had scratched a decade-long itch. *But if New York City is this fabulous*, I thought, *then what else have I been missing out on?*

Falling in love with the city coincided, to the day, with falling in love with Josh. And falling in love with Josh coincided, give or take a year, with falling in love with travel. Prior to meeting him that night at The Ritz, I hadn't seen much of the world: I had flown to Mexico on a family holiday and to South Africa for a musical theatre tour – in other words, I thought of myself as a serious international traveller by American standards. Then Josh sauntered into my life. When we started dating, he showed me his passports, Australian and French, both filled to the brim with so many different stamps that I lost count of the countries he'd been to. I realised that if I stayed with him, I was definitely going to see the world.

As our relationship grew more serious, we would daydream about relocating to London or Paris or Rio or Tokyo. But the most consistent fantasy, the one I brought up every few months, was of moving to Sydney, Australia, the city where Josh was born. I was excited about the possibility of living abroad someday. My mother had lived internationally in her teenage years, and I was fascinated by her stories and confident her experiences with other cultures made her much more interesting than the adults who had never left our town.

The first time we spoke seriously about moving to Australia was the first time Josh took me home to meet his family and friends, in 2012. It started off quite playful. I'd say things like 'I could get used to burgers this big,' or 'If we live here one day, I'll come to this beach every morning.' But after a few days, I was genuinely imagining myself living there. Josh was so relaxed at home, his accent becoming thicker and his energy more at peace. I saw him in a totally different light, learning more about him through his interactions with friends and his favourite childhood places. I knew I was falling in love again – this time with his country.

'Where exactly would we live, monkey?' I asked as he drove me around his childhood neighbourhood of Balmain.

'Is it easy for an American to just move here, or would we need to be married?' I asked as we fell asleep on our final night.

Australia was easy to fall in love with, what with her gorgeous beaches, amazing coffee and lack of guns. Each time I returned to the country, I genuinely considered the move.

A twink in front of the Sydney Harbour Bridge on their very first trip to Australia.

Then in 2016, as we planned to become parents while watching Donald Trump's election campaign unfold, I said to Josh, only half-jokingly, 'If he wins, we're moving to Australia.'

'I'll hold you to that,' Josh replied.

The truth is, our time in Los Angeles was terrible. We'd moved there from New York because I wanted one final adventure before we started our life as parents. Josh wanted to move straight to Sydney, but I begged for a slower transition, and we agreed to give it a try. Sadly, the adventure wasn't a pleasant one. We had best friends living in the city, but Josh hated the traffic, didn't find the scenery inspiring and, worst of all, was struggling to find work that kept him fulfilled. This caused friction in our relationship, because I was thriving. My Paleo diet and addiction to cycling kept me fit and healthy, and I was working with huge clients at times, like Spotify and YouTube. But compromise is part of any good relationship.

Josh was being courted by Australia's public broadcaster for jobs he'd always dreamed of having. After a late-night emotional outburst in June 2017, one of only two times that I had seen my husband cry, we decided – together – that it was time to give Australia a shot. He thought there was a small window of opportunity in his career that he couldn't pass up. And because I planned to stay at home and raise our kids, following in my mother's footsteps, I didn't need to live anywhere specific as long as Josh could bring home the bacon. He had spent a decade in my backyard, and it was time for me to spend a decade in his.

★

Obviously, the decision wasn't an easy one for me. While I had spoken enthusiastically for years about calling Australia home, I still had to convince myself that it was the right move for our soon-to-be family of four. It sounded fun in theory, but what about in reality? At the advice of my therapist, I made a list of pros and cons.

Pros: New experience, living abroad, Josh's dream job and mental health, learning more about Josh's culture, raising children in a safer country, better weather, great cafe culture, using my NYC/LA experience to jump the ladder in a smaller advertising market.

Cons: Not having support from my family as I raise children, no friendship group of my own, starting over with my career, culture shock, lack of comfort food, making my family sad.

The pros outweighed the cons – didn't they? As I stared at the list, I was left with the strong feeling that this decision would break my mother's heart. I knew it might be an impossible pill for her to swallow, and because our relationship had never really been tested like this – not with grandchildren on the line – I became quite anxious.

My mother was raised in Florida in the 1960s and 70s. She and her family moved around a lot because of her stepfather's job, jumping from Illinois to Pittsburgh and then New Jersey, all before she turned fifteen. She then moved to London, England, with her younger brother, Eddy, and her mother, Ofe. Uniquely, the four children – she had two older brothers – were divided into pairs. The older siblings chose to stay in Florida with their father, meaning Mom only got to see the three of them twice a year on short holidays. Her young adulthood was a long series of goodbyes.

My mother met my father in London, while he was studying abroad. They were only friends at first, but it was soon obvious to both of them that they had a special connection. My father was calm and caring, emotionally gentle yet physically strong. Plus, he loved sports as much as she did, so they clicked. The following year, Mom graduated from high school and decided to go to the school Dad attended in America: New England College. The day she landed in Boston, 5 February 1981, he picked her up from the airport, drove her to New Hampshire, took her out to dinner and asked her to be his girlfriend.

Mom left her family behind to fly across the world. She fell in love with a wonderful man in a state she had never been to before, got married shortly after, then stepped away from work for a decade to raise three kids. Phone calls and travel were much more expensive than they are today, so she didn't talk to or get to see her family as often as she would have liked, but she created a life that she loved with a man who adored her. She took a risk, putting herself and the excitement of a new adventure above being physically close to her loved ones. And it seemed that the risk paid off: happy husband, happy children, happy life.

The parallels were uncanny: I was about to move to a faraway country with a man I adored and the prospect of fatherhood on the horizon. It was terribly daunting, but if she could do it, then what was stopping me from doing the same thing?

★

My mother and I spoke on the phone every evening, a habit that I only learned was unusual when I moved to New York and realised that most adults stopped calling so frequently when they moved out. But she was my security blanket, the only person in my life at the time who knew exactly how to manage my anxiety. I told her absolutely everything – some might even say too much. Every boyfriend, every experiment with drugs, and every major and minor mistake was on our daily agenda.

Recently, for the first time in our relationship, I had been keeping a secret from her: the knowledge that I had agreed, nearly a month prior, to relocate my family all the way around the world. When I finally gained confidence in the decision and realised I was running out of time, what with the twins two months from being born, I decided to rip off the bandaid.

On a Friday evening in July 2017, I was walking back to our apartment from my office on Hollywood Boulevard when I made the call. 'Mom, I have something to tell you,' I said sheepishly as I paced back and forth in front of our building. 'I don't know how you're going to react, so I'm just going to blurt it out. We're moving to Australia.'

There was silence on the other end of the line, so I just kept talking to fill the air.

'Josh got a job offer at the ABC in Sydney.'

'He must be excited,' said Mom, clearly doing her best to keep the conversation light.

'It's really his dream job, so we're definitely freaking out a bit.'

'When are you thinking this might happen?' she asked politely.

'We don't have all the details sorted out just yet, but it looks like December.'

'Of next year? That's a good amount of time to get comfort–'

'No, this December. Four months away.'

She fell silent again.

'It's definitely faster than I would have liked,' I said, pre-emptively combating her concerns. 'But Josh has been unhappy in LA, so I think it's worth giving it a shot. It might not be forever, or even for more than a year – who knows, really? It's hard, but it's the right decision for us right now.' I realised I was rambling. I paused, waiting for her reaction, my heart beating out of my chest. I had been preparing for this moment for weeks.

She cleared her throat, took a deep breath and said, 'I'm very happy for you two.' Then she told me she had to go and make dinner, and she hung up the phone.

We didn't speak for three days. That is a catastrophically long period of time when you usually talk to someone every single day. I called my father to check she was okay, and he suggested I just give her some space. 'She needs some time to process the news,' he said.

But I desperately needed her approval. She had walked this path before me. In many ways, the reason I felt so confident in my ability to follow in her footsteps was that she had been so successful. If I struggled in Australia, she would provide all of the answers as my guide, my mentor, my mother. I needed her to tell me that I was going to be okay, even if I wasn't. But she simply couldn't give me that – not in the moment, at least.

The lack of communication was turning me inside out. Instead of focusing on the massive tasks at hand, I became consumed by thoughts of what my mother was thinking. I couldn't sleep, I stopped eating, and I was a broken record with Josh and all of our friends. Mom had a right to take some time to process the news, but did she really need five entire days? I was worried that this silent treatment was an indication of what was to come.

On the sixth day, I called her. Within seconds, it was clear she was very emotional. She apologised for the waterworks, then said she needed to be honest with me. I had anticipated this, so sat back and buckled up for the ride.

She presented me with a laundry list of questions that she said she hoped I had answers for. 'Does Josh have friends with children who live there?' 'Is there a parenting group in the neighbourhood you plan to move to?' 'Have you connected with a local GP?' 'Will you see a therapist when you arrive?' 'Will you work or be a stay-at-home father?' 'Have you checked out the local day cares or found nearby nannies?' 'Will you have your own car?' 'Will you have your own money?'

In retrospect, all of her questions were ones I should have asked myself before agreeing to move. To give myself some credit, I *had* softly addressed a majority of her concerns with Josh, but that was after he had accepted the job offer. Now her questions piled up on my shoulders, and instead of hearing the cautious motherly love in her voice, I thought she was making a direct attack on our decision to move. I even wondered if she was trying to manipulate me into staying in America.

To be honest, I wasn't ready to face the reality of what lay ahead. But I was finding it far too stressful to take on the weight of what could go wrong in Australia, considering my history with mental illness and the addition of twins. I suppressed my fears in order to avoid a vicious anxiety loop that had hurt me many times when large decisions needed to be made. I was capable of derailing any good opportunity by plotting its demise, so I didn't need my mother's help in doing so. Call it denial, but I'd been drowning out the negativity with a soundtrack of naive positivity. I wanted to start my parenting journey on a high, believing I could tackle it all. Sadly, Mom was getting in the way of that.

One night, she talked through problems that could arise if Josh and I broke up while living abroad, and I snapped at her. 'You think it's fucking easy for me to sit here day after day and listen to you bitch on the phone to me like I'm not the person who's causing you all of this pain? Instead of supporting me like a mother should support her son, you're thinking of every reason why I shouldn't go. Well, the decision has been made. We're going. If you can't deal with that, then we need to stop talking.'

My mother had direct experience with the journey I was about to embark on. She felt, maybe justifiably, that it was her duty to prepare me for reality – not just as her son, but as the father of her grandchildren. But I felt like she was projecting a lot of her issues with her past experiences onto me. She thought the best person to work through her issues with my move was me; I thought that person should be a therapist. She wanted to make sure I was prepared if something went wrong, and I wanted to focus on everything going right.

My outburst was a line in the sand for our relationship. Our conversations continued, but our dynamic shifted. We only spoke two days a week, and usually we kept the calls short.

Some were great, with Mom giving me the positive support I was looking for, but others went badly. I withheld information from her, especially about my feelings towards moving. Our calls became flat and emotionless, lacking the depth we were used to.

When I think back to the few months before I became a father, I don't think of them fondly. Instead of preparing to make a seamless transition, I was consumed by what I saw as my mother's disappointment. I had decided that she didn't support my plan to move to Australia, which meant she didn't support me. But I had plans, unbeknown to her, to make her proud. I was going to be the exact type of parent that she had been for me. I was going to step away from work, like she had. I was going to manage the home, like she had. I was going to be crafty and clever and cook up a storm, just like she had. I just hadn't planned on doing it without her support.

Chapter Six

The Twin Towers

Our packed bags were by the front door: two small hard-shell suitcases parked side by side, with a carry-on duffle full of baby clothes delicately balanced on top. Sara lived an hour from the Mayo Clinic in Rochester, where our twins would be born. Josh and I lived thirty minutes from the airport, which was a three hour and twenty-five minute flight from the Minneapolis airport, which was an hour and eighteen minute drive from the hospital. Rather than moving to Minnesota a month before the due date, which we had considered, we'd agreed to wait in LA until Sara began going into labour. This would be her fourth birth, and she felt confident she'd be able to give us ample warning. At the smallest of labour signs, we'd be on the next flight.

During the drama with my mother, Josh suggested that we end our lease and move in with my parents for two months before flying off to Australia. This would give them a chance to connect with the twins, and hopefully give me and Mom a chance to mend our fences. I agreed. We now needed as much time as possible to pack and sell our belongings before the birth, and that was the main reason why we didn't spend a month in Minnesota.

Sara texted us on Sunday morning, 10 September 2017. I scurried around our flat, unplugging cords and packing laptops and toiletries, while Josh booked us on the earliest flight out of LAX. We ordered an Uber, which took much longer to arrive than any other Uber ever had. I said a quick goodbye to our apartment, never to return.

As the car sped along Sunset Boulevard, Josh and I held each other's hands tight with unprecedented anticipation. I needed to roll down the window and force more air into my lungs. The excitement was palpable as we shared the news with our driver. 'Our surrogate is in labour – we'll be fathers soon!' It was unlike any nervous energy we had ever experienced; as though we were floating above the car, watching the movie of our lives.

Soon after we arrived at LAX, Sara and Nate let us know they'd arrived at the Mayo Clinic. Luckily we had in-flight wi-fi and could continue the conversation. Sara sat in the hospital waiting room for much longer than I thought appropriate for a human about to give birth to twins. Four hours later, or maybe it was just fourteen minutes, she was finally meeting with our doctor. I expected the medical staff to rush her into a birthing suite so that she could relax, but instead they sent her home. Our saint of a surrogate had been kicked out onto the cold streets of Rochester at nightfall.

Sara explained to us, less dramatically, that while she felt heavy contractions close together, she was less than three centimetres dilated, so the staff had suggested that she drive home and maybe come back the next day. Every selfish part of us wanted this to be true. We'd have time to land, drive to our hotel and check in, and we'd get some sleep before the babies were born. Josh – knowing that Sara lived an hour from the hospital and not feeling comfortable with the thought of her having an emergency birth in the car – booked her and Nate a hotel room across the street from the Mayo Clinic.

We landed around 11 pm. We dashed over to the rental car lot, and I yelled at Josh the second I saw the vehicle. 'Are you crazy? We're a family of four now – we need a much bigger car!' But time was of the essence, so I lost the midnight battle and we began the hour-long drive.

Just as we pulled out of the lot, we received a text from Nate that said they were back in hospital. Sara's contractions were getting stronger, and as a veteran of the birthing game she knew 'something was happening soon'. Thank god we'd all trusted our instincts: it turned out she was ten centimetres dilated.

When Josh and I were about twenty minutes from the Mayo Clinic, Nate began sending us more messages. *We need to go now,* the first one read, followed by, *How close are you?* and finally, *C-section.* We were quiet, tense. Right at the speed limit as we drove through the dark. Trying to sound unruffled to each other. Hoping that we would arrive in time. Hoping that Sara was taken care of and that the twins were okay.

At 1.57 am on 11 September, we were exactly six minutes away when we received a text from Nate saying, *It's a boy!* Cooper Steven Szeps. A millisecond later, a photo of our son being held by the nursing staff came through. And exactly one minute after that, another text arrived with a picture of another infant: *It's a girl!* Stella Rose Szeps.

We were screaming with excitement in the car. Josh gleefully banged his hands on the steering wheel, and I rolled down the window to yell, 'We're fathers!' just as we peeled around the corner towards the hospital entrance.

Before stopping the car, Josh turned to me and said, 'Given it's 9/11, we should probably get the twin tower jokes out of the way before we go in there.'

We parked illegally, right in front of the Mayo Clinic, and rushed up to the sliding front doors – which, dramatically, did not open. We were darting around outside the hospital, searching for anyone inside, jumping and waving our arms, but the front foyer was empty.

Josh found an emergency call button beside the front door and tapped it aggressively, as if writing in Morse code, *Open the fucking door.*

'How can I help you?' a gentle voice requested.

Josh yelled into the box, holding back tears. 'We're fathers! We just had babies! Our twins! Our children were just born here!'

'Opening the door now – come in, come in!' she urgently replied.

We heard a click. As the door slid open, we rushed into the foyer with no idea where to turn. We ran like madmen through the halls, desperately searching for signs with the words *delivery* or *baby* or *dads from LA, your twins are right here*. Finally we made our way to the obstetrics ward. A pair of nurses greeted us, both with massive smiles on their faces. They signed us in, gave us matching white wristbands, and whisked us over to our own

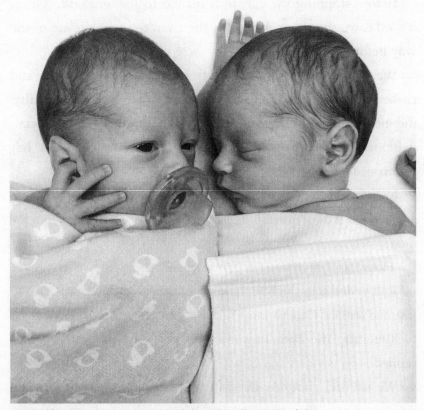

Our babies. That's Cooper on the left and Stella on the right.

delivery room, where we sat holding hands and crying, drunk
with gleeful anticipation.

It was then that we found out something had gone very
wrong. The nursing staff informed us that while we'd been
driving down the I-94 to the hospital, a placental abruption had
occurred: Cooper's placenta had separated early from the uterus.
The staff let us know that an abruption can result in serious
and even deadly consequences. It isn't known exactly why they
happen, and they are hard to spot. We were told that one of the
doctors on duty, who wasn't supposed to be on the floor that
night, noticed the signs – and that a few months earlier, the same
doctor had been present when an abruption was caught 'too late'.

In response to our frantic questions, the staff told us that
not only was Sara okay, but that Cooper would be too. He was
simply being monitored, and he and his sister would be joining
us shortly. Stella would be brought in first.

We waited. It was only five minutes, but it might as well
have been five days. I paced the room, watching as Josh stared
at the floor, both of us desperate to see and touch and smell our
babies – desperate to unite our family of four.

'Here you go, Dads!' A nurse popped into the room, holding
a tiny bundle wrapped in a white cotton blanket with light pink
and blue stripes. 'Who wants to take her first?'

'My husband will,' I blurted out, not giving Josh a chance to
reply. I had planned to give him that special moment with Stella
all along.

While he held her, seated on a bench at the back of the room,
I took pictures and wiped tears from my eyes. And then it was
my turn to hold our baby girl.

The very second I stretched out my right hand and touched the side of Stella's head for the first time, I felt an unexpected sadness lift out of my body. I had spent so many months – years, really – living in a constant state of anticipation. I had planned for this moment, yearned for this moment, paid for this moment. I'd written and talked and sung about it to anyone who would listen. I had dreamt about having a baby, workshopping each potential way that we might meet. But somewhere along this winding road, I had forgotten about eleven-year-old Sean: that little Catholic boy from Concord, New Hampshire, who had discovered he was gay and then, in an instant, suppressed the dream of becoming a father one day. When I held Stella in my hands for the first time, the deep pain I had carried for nearly two decades rose up into the air for me to see again.

This moment hadn't even been an option for my younger self. There was no hope, not even a glimmer of it. There was no one, not a single person, to prove this might be possible. Nothing for him to hold on to. Somewhere along the way, he decided never to dream about it. The sadness of missing out on what he saw as a fundamental human experience got replaced, as it so often does, with all the things we bury on top of the things we hope to ignore.

The gravity of the moment became crystal clear to me. This powerful introduction was not just for us but also for all of the gay men who had never got this chance – the men who faked relationships, who remained single, who had to stay closeted, who found love but couldn't become dads, who took their own lives because the suffering was too intense. The ones who were born in the right body but at the wrong place and time in history.

I said to Josh and the nursing staff, 'How lucky are we?' While it might have sounded like the emotional cry of every first-time parent, mine had many more layers than most. This luck was genuinely rare. Until recently, gay men had found ways to have children under very unique and very secretive circumstances. They hadn't been out and proud, walking into the hospital hand in hand with their partners to deliver their babies.

In that moment, I felt as though all the fighting our community had done, over many decades and lifetimes, had been worth it. Josh and I were one of the relatively few couples in the world (and in history) to create a family like ours, but we wouldn't be the last. Centuries of missed opportunities had maybe, just maybe, come to an end.

Cooper arrived about an hour later, wires streaming from every inch of his body. We had our skin-to-skin moment, him and I, draping the various red and blue cords on either side of me. I fell asleep with him, my baby boy, on my chest. As I closed my eyes, I thought about his middle name, Steven, a named shared by my brother and my father. Unless he eventually told me otherwise, I would be raising a boy, part of the next generation of Gallerani men. I wasn't a stain on my family, a terrible sinner, the one who couldn't make it happen.

After many hours of countless cuddles, Josh and I handing the twins back and forth between us, a nurse invited me to the crafts centre down the hall while Josh slept with the twins. The craft room had a rotating list of activities to keep parents, especially those with children in the Neonatal Intensive Care Unit, entertained. Or maybe distracted. It was an opportunity to do some activities with other new parents, an unexpected invitation that I joyfully accepted. I wrote my children's names on Welcome Home cards, then joined the exhausted people seated all around me.

One woman, a Hispanic mother, introduced herself. 'Hello,' she said quietly.

'Hi there, how are you?' I offered back in a whisper.

'A little out of it,' she said with a giggle.

'Oh, I can imagine. Congratulations!'

'Thank you. Is your wife resting?' she politely asked.

'Oh, no. My husband is in the room with our kids.'

'I'm so sorry, of course. My mind is loopy.'

'Don't worry, I understand. Is this your first?'

'No, no, I have two others – this is my third daughter.'

'Three daughters? Must be a very vibrant house. You can teach me a thing or two.'

'Or maybe you can teach me,' she replied, both of us giggling now. 'Is this your first child?'

'Yes, first and second. We have twins.'

'Twins? Two boys? Two girls?'

'One boy and one girl.'

'Oh, what a miracle. God blessed you with two beautiful gifts. God has His eyes on you and your husband. God bless you and God bless your family.'

★

I was raised Roman Catholic. I wasn't a nominal or cafeteria Catholic, the ones who say they're religious but pick and choose what to believe on any given day of the week: I was a devout Christian who came from a devout family, with a deep connection to Jesus Christ.

Like so many other young Catholics, I attended Mass every Sunday with my family. I also attended Sunday school, learning the basics of my faith. I was a Eucharistic Minister, a person who assists the priest during Mass, and a member of the church choir. I performed in the church's musical for ten years and was one of the three wise men in the annual Christmas nativity performance. I went to youth group retreats as I got older, attended church dances, and collected a majority of my childhood friends from the musty old halls of the Immaculate Heart of Mary.

In short, being Roman Catholic was a major part of my childhood and adolescence. At a time when I knew very little about myself or the world outside of my small-ish town, being a member of that community was integral to who I was and how I saw everything. Nothing was more important to me than being a Gallerani and a Catholic.

Because God loves everyone equally, even with all of our flaws, I felt at peace as a member of His community. I felt at peace as His son. There's extreme joy and comfort in believing that you're on a path to everlasting love. When you're a child and all the adults are saying that you can live forever in Heaven, the most sublime place you could ever imagine, you sprint towards the light. I drank the Communion juice, ate the wafers, wore the cross, bought the t-shirt and played the music in my car on repeat. I sprinted, with glee, towards a future that seemed perfect. That is, until I began to realise I was gay.

I was sitting with a group of older friends in the church basement, gossiping before our first rehearsal of a musical revue. One of the older girls, I'll call her Siobhan★, was reading a piece of laminated yellow paper. There was no writing on the back, but I was interested to see what it was. As it made its way closer to me via the hands of all the other kids sitting in a circle, their reactions – some of shock and others of amusement – made me giddy with anticipation.

'What's a homosexual?' one of the boys whispered.

'A gay person,' Siobhan replied in a light and matter-of-fact tone.

Everybody laughed. I forced a laugh, too.

'Like Sean!' another boy called out, instantly silencing the group.

'Don't say that – he's just a kid,' Siobhan chimed in, giving me a don't-mind-him look.

'I was only joking,' he said, while the paper continued to be passed around the circle.

I smiled and forced another unnecessary laugh, wishing desperately that the yellow card wouldn't make its way to me – that instead, an earthquake would hit and swallow it up. But a few seconds later, the card landed in my lap. I searched for the word as if my life depended on it. And there it was: *HOMOSEXUALITY.* It was seven bullet points down from title, *OVERT SINS,* and sandwiched between *BESTIALITY* and *PEDERASTY.*

'God bless those poor people,' Siobhan said with a sigh, addressing the whole circle.

'Yeah, God bless them,' I quietly replied.

I didn't know what all those words meant, but one thing had just become abundantly clear. There was a word out there in the world, a very bad word, that meant 'gay'. And whatever gay was, it was a sin. And I was, according to at least one member of that group of older kids, probably gay: Sean Gallerani, a sinner, in deep need of God's blessing.

★

I was sitting in the craft room at the Mayo Clinic, only a few short feet away from where my newborn babies were fast asleep with my husband in the delivery room. I had been a father for less than twenty-four hours, and I was staring at a stranger who had offered me and my new family God's blessing, a blessing I didn't want.

In the past, phrases like this had triggered me, sending me into weeks-long spirals of ruminating on my religious trauma. Whenever someone offered me God's blessing, I was always sucked right back in. To them, it was a harmless and polite expression, often given little thought. It would never have crossed their minds that someone might be negatively affected – after all, a blessing is delivered with grace and kindness. But I wanted nothing to do with God. Whenever a religious person delivered the blessing with religious intent, I would pull out one of my many sassy replies, hoping to challenge their way of thinking: 'I'm glad *you* believe that' or 'Please pass along my thanks to *your* God for me.' On that day, 11 September 2017, I changed. I was a father now, no longer the star of my story. I had always been an ego-driven individual, my anxiety demanding this of me. Today a new voice had entered the chatroom: a kinder, warmer, more empathetic perspective that was not affected by my religious trauma. Sure, it would have been easy – fun, even – to remind this woman that her beliefs weren't the only ones that existed, but what kind of message did I want to send to Stella and Cooper? Was that how I would speak in front of them?

I turned to her and said, 'Thank you so much for your kind words.'

She smiled back at me, picked up her Welcome Home card and walked out of the room. As she did, I reflected on the cosmic shift I had just felt inside of me.

If my kids had been old enough to understand, I would have told them, 'Some people believe in God, a supreme creator who made everything we see and know. But some people, like Dada, do not. It's important that we respect people for their differences, especially when they are trying to respect us. I don't believe in that woman's God, but I understand that "May God bless you" is her way of saying, "I hope you have a wonderful life." And that, my dears, is a wonderful thing to say.' I sat there smiling, proud of myself. Dealing with religious trauma would remain a constant struggle in my life, I knew that. But today it had less of a nasty grip on my happiness than it had the day prior, and that was worth celebrating.

As I picked up my newly decorated Welcome Home signs and walked out of the craft room and back to my family, I thought, *If this is what I've learnt on Day One of being a dad, what's the rest of this roller-coaster ride going to deliver?*

Chapter Seven

The Mïni Period

I was afraid of vaginas back then. If someone had asked me to rank my comfort with female genitalia on a scale of one to ten, I probably would have given it a three. I knew how the female reproductive system worked, and I could have pointed to a clitoris on an anatomy chart. But the exit and entrance of various objects and substances simply wasn't my forte.

So you can imagine the genuine horror I experienced when, less than twenty-four hours after I became a parent, a delivery nurse nonchalantly told me, 'Stella might bleed down there in the next few days. It's not a big deal – just think of it like a mini period. Clean it like you normally would, and she'll be fine.'

As soon as the term 'mini period' fell from her mouth, I lost my hearing. Okay, that's a slight exaggeration, but it sure as hell felt like it. My heart raced, the room began spinning, and the nurse's words became muffled like those of an adult in a Peanuts cartoon. I was looking at her lips, valiantly trying to focus on her vagina briefing but unable to comprehend anything coming out of her well-intentioned mouth.

Even though I was smiling – one of those forced grins you see in class portraits of primary school students – I wasn't fooling anyone. My anxious monkey brain was doing mental gymnastics so intense that Simone Biles, the greatest gymnast ever to live, would have accepted defeat. If my husband hadn't been sleeping with Cooper on his chest, he would have seen the signs of me losing the plot and jumped in to rescue me. But alas, I was alone.

'A mini period?' I said to the nurse. 'I don't understand how to deal with a regular period, let alone a mini one. Actually, I don't know how to clean a vagina at all. What the hell is a "normal clean"? Are there different levels of cleaning for vaginas?'

I've made a massive mistake having a daughter, I thought to myself. *Why did I think it would be possible to raise a girl when my gay-ass husband and I know literally nothing about all of this? This is why straight people say we shouldn't have kids. Maybe they were right all along – maybe we can't do this. We need a woman. My daughter needs a mom. I'm already failing. I'm a stupid piece of–*

An unfamiliar sound broke through my self-destructive inner monologue. Stella, my daughter, was crying. It was one of those 'I've only been alive for twenty-four hours and am just testing things out' sort of whinges, but the soft sound triggered something I hadn't felt before. She needed me. She needed us. She didn't know or care about our sex or gender. This helpless, angelic creature just needed someone to care for her. No one else was going to clean her vagina for her. No one else was going to change her nappy. No one else was going to explain her anatomy to her in an age-appropriate way, or support her through nasty cramps and buy her tampons when the time came: that was our job now.

I scooped her up and held her close to my chest, realising my experience with vaginas – or lack thereof – was irrelevant. Was I disappointed in my useful-knowledge deficit? Abso-fucking-lutely. Was I uncomfortable with how much I needed to learn and how quickly it needed to be done? You bet your ass I was. But nine months ago I had made a commitment to this baby girl, and I planned on following through with it. I was going to educate myself as quickly as possible. I was going to ask questions, read books, speak with my husband – speak with anyone who was willing to listen – and I wasn't going to stop until I felt that Josh and I were confident in our knowledge of female biology. This was our responsibility.

Strangely, I felt relieved. I took a deep breath, turned to the nurse and spoke calmly. 'Listen, I don't have a lot of experience with vaginas. I need you to rewind and walk me through all of this again, starting with whatever a "normal clean" is.'

She hesitated, her eyes on my daughter. Her pregnant pause made it clear that this was uncharted territory for her, too, which put me at ease. She collected herself and looked up at me while gently placing her hand on my shoulder. 'That's my mistake, sir. I'm so sorry. Most dads have their wives in the room when we talk about this kind of stuff ... and, honestly, their eyes usually glaze over. I was on autopilot.'

'Don't worry,' I said, holding back tears. 'I just want to do this right.'

As my family and I continued to rest and recuperate in the hospital, I couldn't stop thinking about my new responsibility. And the longer I spent considering the list of traditionally mom-centric activities that I felt unprepared to administer, the clearer it became that, in general, men were being left out or opting out – both actively and accidentally – of key elements in young children's lives. And by 'key elements', I really mean their private parts. It seemed that the maintenance and upkeep of babies bodies had been placed firmly into mum's corner and dads were asked to steer clear of it. We were obviously making progress. Dads were now encouraged to be in the delivery room and knew they had to change nappies. But although times had changed, our level of understanding of one another's sex characteristics – important biological features of the children we were raising – had not.

When we left the hospital, I was fired up and ready to go on a quest for knowledge.

★

For days after that incident, I became obnoxiously obsessed with the subject. I do this a lot, getting hooked on a topic and then forcing everyone within earshot to engage in a longwinded discussion about it.

Naturally I started by talking with Josh, but he was no help. Not in a bad way – he just knew as much as I did. And he was much more pragmatic about the situation, confident that the women in our lives would look out for us: 'We have your mom, your sister, my mum and all of our female friends. If we have questions, they will happily help.' Even though I knew that was true, I really wanted to form my own understanding of my daughter's needs. I wanted to be the one who looked out for Stella.

I began asking all the men in my life one simple question: 'How much do you know about female anatomy?' The answers were startling. Even the dads of daughters, on average, seemed to understand very little about this subject, let alone how one might clean or care for a vagina. This was surely connected to the lack of appreciation and support that many men were giving to their female counterparts, at home and at work. Was this where inequality began, with babies?

'I know they have periods,' one first-time dad of a daughter told me. 'They use tampons to clean it all up. I think it happens for a few weeks every month, but sometimes they don't have it. My wife can explain it better.'

There it was, clear as day. If someone born with a vagina was available when a question came up specific to their needs, why would a man need to (a) answer it, (b) ask more questions to better understand said question, or (c) follow up and learn more?

This was clearly a problem, not just in my close circle of friends and family, but in our society at large. Relying on humans with vaginas to 'explain it better' was placing too much pressure on them – especially when, in a majority of families, women were already taking on the bulk of parenting responsibilities. And this approach was lacklustre at best when, you guessed it, a modern family had gay dads. There is no 'wife' in our immediate family to 'explain it better', so I made it my mission to become a master at explaining it myself.

I started by making a list of questions specific to my daughter's needs that I wanted answers to – answers that would help make me a better father.

- Do all newborn girls have a mini period?
- Do girls really mature faster than boys, cognitively and physically?
- Do girls develop fine and gross motor skills at different times/levels than boys?
- Are girls better than boys at verbal or non-verbal motor skills?
- Do girls really have more empathy than boys?
- Do girls go through puberty first?
- What is the youngest a girl can go through puberty?
- What comes first: breasts, pubic hair or menstruation?
- How quickly do breasts develop and is it painful?
- Where will hair grow and is it painful?
- Why do some girls have more or less hair than others?
- How long do periods last?
- What causes a period?
- Can/should you take medicine during your period?
- Are tampons the most popular menstrual product?
- Are there more environmentally friendly options?
- What did women do before the invention of tampons?
- When can girls go on birth control?
- What are the effects of going onto birth control?
- What are the signs that a girl has a disease of the reproductive system?
- What are these diseases called, and what is known about them?

The more I learned about my daughter's body, the more I understood her needs. And the more I understood her needs, the closer I felt to her.

With each article I read and video I watched, I felt like I was forging a stronger bond with her, even though she was only a few days old. I knew I would never be able to fully understand the experience of being a woman. But my new knowledge was giving me more empathy for Stella's situation and the challenges she would face in life. In fact, my research expanded my appreciation for women as a whole. Every woman who came before Stella and every woman who would follow.

I started to care deeply about issues I had never before been prompted to think about. What started off as simple Google searches with questions like 'How often do women have periods?' swiftly led to more empathetic searches: 'Are tampons comfortable?' 'Are there less intrusive menstrual products on the market?' 'What period products exist for exercising and swimming?' 'When were tampons invented?' 'What did they do before tampons?' 'Why do we complicate the buying process by having so many menstrual products to choose from?' 'Why are these products so expensive?' 'Do trans men still have periods?' 'Why doesn't the government pay for menstrual products?'

I think all parents should be required to take basic human biology courses. All parents should seriously consider the issues that their children are likely to face based on their gender and sex. When it comes to this aspect of parenthood, no parent should be off the hook.

Chapter Eight

The Cotton Bud

We didn't settle into our new home in Sydney until eighty-four days after Stella and Cooper were earth-side. Their first three days were spent at the Mayo Clinic. I had it in my head that we needed to have as much time alone as possible before allowing visitors. Because of Cooper's dramatic entrance, I wanted to get an official sign-off from the doctors that everything was A-okay before introducing family members into the equation. If we had been physically closer to our families – Josh's parents and brother lived in England, and my family lived in New England – I would have happily opened the hospital doors to them after twenty-four hours, knowing they'd simply drive home after a short visit. Under the circumstances, we would have been hosting a mini family reunion in Minnesota, and I wasn't keen on that. Josh and I agreed to welcome my mom only, knowing she would provide a much-needed pair of hands during our stay in Rochester and flight back to New Hampshire.

I was still quite upset about how Mom had handled the news of us moving to Australia. But when she rocked up to the Mayo Clinic and rushed for me first instead of the babies, I decided to bury the discomfort and lean into the magic of the moment. I wasn't going to let the tension between us ruin the once-in-a-lifetime experience of becoming a father, and I knew she would want the same, for herself and for me. *She'll rise to the occasion,* I told myself. *We'll put the past behind us, at least for now.* I loved seeing her hold the twins for the first time, with tears leaking from her eyes. She kept staring at me and saying, 'You're a daddy now,' and I'd reply, 'And you're an abuela.'

We left the hospital, but we couldn't leave Rochester just yet. Each US state has its own surrogacy laws, differing massively from jurisdiction to jurisdiction. Unlike in Australia, where compensating a surrogate is currently illegal, Minnesota is friendly towards paid surrogacy arrangements. We just needed a post-birth order to be filed with the local court and a hearing to be scheduled. Josh was the biological father, and Sara was, by law, the biological mother; if everything went according to plan that day, she would be removed from the birth certificates and I would adopt the children.

While we waited for the judicial system and the Circle Surrogacy team to work their magic, we bunkered down in a local hotel with my mother. Josh didn't have a lot of experience with babies, so watching him do everything for the first time was pure bliss – and watching him fall in love with our twins unlocked a deeper level of love inside of me. Parenting can drive couples apart or bring them closer together, and luckily the latter happened to us. Josh was also growing closer with

Josh and me leaving the hospital, beaming. The calm before the storm.

Mom. He was hugely grateful to her and felt that she struck the perfect balance of helping without being overbearing. With a constant grin, he soaked up her assistance and gladly accepted suggestions at every milestone.

Josh and I felt like equals, because neither of us had just given birth. We were each able to take full responsibility for one child at a time, alternating babies every half hour or so, and we were both learning to master bottle-feeding and nappy-changing. Because our kids didn't physically need one of us more than the other, there wasn't the 'parenting power imbalance' I had read about, where one parent is forced to do the heavy lifting while the other – the father in most hetero couples – picks up and drops off the child, waiting patiently for their next assignment. Josh and I slept the same amount, fed the twins the same number of times and changed the same number of nappies. That bonded us in a way neither of us had expected. I felt like we were intrepid voyagers who had just landed on a new planet, walking hand in hand as we explored uncharted territory.

On the twelfth day after the birth, we arrived at the Olmsted County District Court. Our surrogate, who said she was healing beautifully and already thinking of going back to work, joined us and a newly appointed lawyer to present our case to a local judge.

I will always remember that day. Sara and Nate were sitting beside us in the courtroom, and Mom was directly behind us with our nappy bag on her lap. Josh and I faced the judge, each with a child in our arms. The judge was a woman in her forties with a pixie haircut and a very serious demeanour. I took a deep, nervous breath as I watched her organise the papers in front of her, each movement deliberate. I'd been told that Minnesota almost always sided with the intended parents, especially when they had entered a legally binding contract with the surrogate prior to the pregnancy, but I was still extremely anxious. It was my first time in court, and I had the strange feeling that I'd done something wrong and was about to go on trial. One of my legs was shaking, my armpits were sweating, and I kept talking to Stella, who had fallen asleep in my arms.

Josh placed his hand on my shaking leg. 'We've made it to the finish line,' he whispered.

And with that, my nerves vanished.

The judge began by asking Sara a series of questions. 'How long have you known Josh and Sean?' 'Have they shown interest in the birth process?' 'Were you forced into this arrangement at any time?' 'Do you think Sean and Josh are suitable fathers for Stella and Cooper?' 'Do you understand that you are giving up legal rights to raising these children?'

Then the tables turned: Josh and I were questioned. 'How long have you two been married?' 'When did you decide to have children?' 'How far away is your family?' 'How often do you communicate with them?' 'Do you understand the responsibility you are undertaking?'

The judge then sat silently and took some notes on a yellow pad. I turned to check in on my mom, each of us wiping tears from our eyes.

After a few minutes, the judge cleared her throat and finally spoke. 'Today is a very good day. I love this job, but oftentimes I look down from this seat at people who are lost. They're struggling, having turned their backs on loved ones or, worse, wishing to separate from them entirely. But then I have days like today, where I get to look down at a sea of people who want to give two children a loving home – a group of people, all of you, who have come together from various parts of the world to give Stella and Cooper a wonderful life. It's a reminder that families come in all shapes and sizes. It's love that defines a family, and I see that in abundance here today. Now how about you all come up here and let's take a picture together.'

Sara snapped the picture of us, with my mom in the middle holding the twins. We thanked the judge, and I left the courtroom as one of the legal fathers of Stella and Cooper Szeps. The complicated surrogacy process had officially and emotionally come to a close. Because I had been driving our journey from the very first day, taking the lead on correspondence with the agency and Sara, a big weight lifted off my shoulders.

I never once felt distanced from my kids or uncomfortable with adopting them, but the kind words from the judge and the knowledge that my name would sit next to Josh's on the birth certificates made a difference to me. There was a sense of total relief. As we walked out into the sunny parking lot, I whispered to Stella, 'I'm officially your dad.'

At our cars we hugged Sara and Nate goodbye, thanking them profusely for the great gifts they had given us and the gifts we would continue to receive. Sara had told us that she planned to pump her breastmilk and donate it to one of the banks located all around America – and Australia, too – to assist parents of premature babies, mothers who struggle to express milk, and motherless families like ours. 'Pumping will also help me lose baby weight and return my uterus to its pre-pregnancy size,' she shared. 'Plus it delays the return of my period, so it's a win-win.' Josh and I leaped at the opportunity to pay her for the milk — at two thousand dollars per month for two months — delighting in the thought of an additional connection to bond us all as a modern family.

The enormity of Sara's strength and selflessness rushed over me as we parted ways. 'We'll never be able to repay you,' I said to her.

'Raising your beautiful kids to the best of your ability is payment enough,' she replied.

And with that, we drove back to our hotel to pack up the room before we headed to the airport. We needed to take two flights: the first from Rochester to Connecticut, and the second from Connecticut to Boston, where my father – who wasn't used to being away from my mother for so long – would be waiting for us. Josh, traveller extraordinaire, had done his research and knew our best chance at a drama-free trip was to book our flights and plan our feedings around take-offs and landings. 'If the babies are latched on to a bottle,' he explained, 'then their ears will continuously pop, avoiding unnecessary meltdowns as the cabin pressure changes.'

Everything worked out according to his master plan. The children drank during take-offs, slept during the flights and drank during landings. 'Whoever said flying with kids was difficult surely didn't know what they were talking about,' I jokingly said to Josh.

'You'll regret saying that one day,' he whispered back, laughing and kissing me as the plane disembarked.

I'll never forget the look in my father's eyes when we met him in the airport. Like my mother, he ignored my babies and rushed towards Mom and me. After he kissed Mom, he met me in an enormous bearhug, whispering, 'I'm so proud of you.' He gazed down at the babies, who were asleep in car seats, and brushed away a tear. We stood there, father and son, his arm on my shoulder. 'I'm so happy you're home, buddy.'

'Me too, Popsicle. Me too.'

★

As soon as we arrived at my parents' home in New Hampshire, we settled into a comfortable routine. My mother brilliantly suggested that we create a sleep schedule, allowing each of the four adults – myself, Josh, Mom and Dad – to work four-hour night shifts, rotating every two days. That meant, shockingly for first-time parents, that Josh and I would be able to get eight hours of sleep per night for the first two months. This allowed us to be present and aware; capable of making sound and rational decisions – a simple pleasure that I would later long for. To this day, it's arguably the greatest gift my parents ever gave me.

Those first two months were filled with epic highs and lows. It was a genuine delight to watch Dad realise how much work the babies were and thank Mom for all she'd done while raising us. He has always been an extremely supportive husband and involved father, but I remember the moment he fully acknowledged her efforts, so many years later. 'I don't know how you managed three kids at once, Sally. I can barely keep track of one.'

Watching my siblings hold the twins for the first time changed me. My little sister, Samantha, decided to use up most of her holiday leave and stay at our parents' home to support us. She was a natural, instantly bonding with the babies and treating them like her own. She took over most of the night shifts while she was visiting, mastered nappy changes and anxiously googled illnesses at the slightest symptom. Watching her rise to the role of tia ('aunt' in Spanish) made us grow even closer. My brother, Steven, had never really held a baby before. He was nervous, unsure if he wanted to hold the twins at all. But when we handed over Cooper for the first time, Steven melted into a puddle. He fell silent as he drew Cooper close to his face, smelling his nephew's forehead. My brother isn't a crier, not like me, but I swore I saw the hint of a tear glistening in the corner of his eye.

Watching my grandmother and grandfather, my mimi and papa, become great-grandparents was a true honour. My papa, who has since passed away, wasn't a very talkative man in his later years, but he said, 'Congratulations', and, 'Are you ready to be a father?' I cried about this in private, knowing it was likely one of the last few times I'd hear his voice.

Watching my best friend, Joe, meet the twins for the first time was powerful. He cried, naturally, then whispered, 'Is it weird if I call you "Daddy" now?' causing both of us to belly laugh and wake the babies.

But my favourite moments, the ones I revisit during times of uncertainty or stress, were when I was watching my husband become a father. One of these moments involved Josh and a cotton bud.

Cooper was, without question, constipated. His face was turning purple as he squeezed and squealed his way through a difficult 48-hour period. During those early days, we had become addicted to monitoring the children's poop schedules, so Josh was first to flag that Cooper was likely clogged up. Luckily, our doctor was on speed dial.

'Is there anything I can do to stop this?' I asked her frantically.

'Honestly, it usually clears itself up,' she said. 'You can increase feedings, massage his stomach and make sure he's getting extra tummy time – but if you're really concerned, you can dip a cotton bud in vaseline and then …'

'Let him lick the vaseline?'

'I guess you could say that.' She laughed. 'Stick it into his rear ever so gently. That should unclog him and give him a bit of relief. It's not standard practice, and I wouldn't suggest you make it a habit, but if you're very concerned … it's a solid Plan D.'

I grabbed the vaseline and a box of cotton buds, then handed them over to Josh, who has a much stronger stomach for poop and blood than I do. He sat Cooper, barely one month old, on the baby-changing station that my father had set up at the window facing the lake. Josh lifted Cooper's legs in the air, softly pressed the head of the cotton bud into his bum, and pulled it out almost immediately.

'Is it working?' I asked nervously.

'I don't think so. Did she say how far to push it?'

'She said, "Ever so gently" – I wrote that down – but she didn't say how far. Should we call her back?' I was feeling anxious. 'Let me call her back.'

'It's fine, don't call her back just yet. We can do this – I can do this. I'll try it again, this time a tad further in.'

One of the best parts of being a parent, as we all know, is watching your newborn baby smile after having his anal passage cleared with a cotton bud.

Josh went ahead with this plan. When he pulled the cotton bud out, diarrhoea spurted from Cooper's bum. It sprayed across Josh's shirt, his chin and the wall behind him.

We stared for a few seconds in disbelief, watching as the colour in Cooper's face shifted from purple to red and back to beige. Josh looked me in the eye and just said, 'Well, shit.' This was met with uncontrollable laughter that lasted for days. If I was going to have to deal with the shitty parts of parenting, I was happy it was with him.

During those two months I felt relieved that I had trapped Josh into marrying my ass, thanking my lucky stars that Kris had taken me to The Ritz. Whenever things were stressful with the twins or my family, Josh remained calm and rational. He gave me permission to trust my gut. When we were met with problems – like how best to thaw breastmilk in the middle of the night – he'd go away for an hour, develop a system and then train the rest of the family to ensure we were all on the same page. He had entered the parenting experience without his family, moving in with his in-laws for two months, but he never once let that discomfort show. When I complained or got anxious, he took the pressure off of my shoulders and placed it onto his own. 'I've got you,' he'd say. And I knew that he did. This meant that, as we continued preparing for the big move to Australia, I was able to – mostly – ignore the nerves, knowing I had a solid rock of a husband to support me.

★

A few weeks before the move, Josh and I agreed that he would go to Sydney for a week to get things in order. We'd need a car, we'd need furniture, and we'd need to sign a rental contract on the home we had found online and had only seen via a video tour. We'd need nappies. We'd need new mobile phones. And I'm sure there was a long list of other things for him to sort out.

While my husband was abroad, the conversation that had been bubbling up for months and months finally occurred between me and Mom during one of our night-shift handovers. Maybe it happened because Josh wasn't there, or because our time in New Hampshire was more than halfway over. As my mother and I sat there in silence, with the twins asleep in a cot on the floor, she finally addressed the elephant in the room.

'Do you think we'll be able to get back to where we were before?'

I could have pretended not to understand her question, but we both knew what she meant. Even though I hated to admit it, we were wired the same way. I knew, deep in my bones, that she had spent every minute we'd sat there in silence – and probably every day for the past two months – replaying the events that had transpired all those months ago.

'I don't know,' I replied honestly, meeting her gaze.

'I really did try my best.'

'Me too.'

That night I told her exactly how I felt, unloading a monologue that I had internally workshopped for months in anticipation of this moment. It poured out of me in a hushed whisper, floating over the sleeping twins.

Mom remained silent. She just sat there and took it, as I had taken her line of questions during those months before the children were born.

When I was finished, we sat in tears across from one another as she apologised. And then I apologised, too. I think we both knew we had handled the situation less than perfectly, but it was in that conversation that I came to learn just how hard it had been for her to watch me make a decision so similar to the one she had struggled with for many years.

'I asked the questions that I wished someone had asked me back then,' she said. 'But too many, too frequently and without considering how you would feel to hear them all from the person you most wanted support from. I just wanted you to be prepared.'

'And I just wanted you to be proud of me.'

'I'll always be proud of you.'

Two days later, Josh returned to help us pack our belongings before we flew to Australia. As I filled up the last suitcase, my mother watched the twins in the living room in silence.

The final goodbye was difficult for everyone. Just before we left, Mom handed me a letter in an envelope and asked me to read it when I was settled in Sydney. 'It's everything I can't say to you right now.'

I couldn't wait. I opened the letter on the plane.

Dear Sean, it began. *I did the best I could ...*

As I finished reading the letter, I looked out the window and sobbed, wishing I could hug her one last time. I felt a deep connection to her, as though I could feel the anxiety of her maiden voyage to America, all those years ago, pulsing through me while I made my own journey to a new life overseas. I finally understood her reaction to my announcement, and the questions she'd asked, and the tears that had fallen during so many of our calls.

I held that letter close to my chest, pushing it into my skin, wishing with every inch of my being that we could have a do-over. I wanted my mommy back.

*

We flew together as a family from Boston to New York, New York to Seoul, and Seoul to Sydney. The stopovers were part of the trip because I had demanded that Josh wield his travel-hacking superpowers to book us first-class flights all the way there using frequent flyer miles. I was overwhelmed at the thought of flying with newborn babies in economy, and I also really liked the idea of marking this emotional journey as a once-in-a-lifetime special occasion, worthy of premium seats.

I had prepared little bags of lollies for the long-haul flights, ones that also contained handwritten letters 'from the twins' to the other first-class passengers – people who had bought $20,000 airfares, not expecting that they would be seated next to a pair of newborns. The letters, written in both English and Korean, read: *Dear fellow passenger, we'd like to apologise in advance for any noises we might make during this flight. We're only two months old. Please enjoy these chocolates as a small gesture of compensation. Hopefully, this makes up for any disruption to your flight. Sincerely yours – Stella and Cooper (newborns).*

After eighty days out of the womb and nearly thirty-three hours of travel, the twins finally arrived in the city where we planned to raise them. The second we got off the plane, we were met with a blast of humid summer heat, the polar opposite of the snowy New Hampshire weather we had just left behind – a fierce and forceful reminder that things would never be the same.

For the first five days in Sydney, before our rental house became available, we stayed at the home of old family friends. Josh's parents were still living in the UK but, to our relief, were preparing to move back to Sydney in a few months.

I pretended I was okay with it all, but arriving in a foreign country with two newborns and no home or family was deeply upsetting to me. To make matters worse, the shipping company had stuffed up: it turned out that our belongings hadn't made the crate in time and would take – get this – three months longer than expected. We were eighty-two days post-birth. I didn't have a home, I didn't have my family, and now I didn't have my belongings.

'I can't get over the feeling that this was all a mistake,' I said to Josh one humid night as we lay beside each other in a sticky room with no fan or air-con. 'We're months into being parents, and we don't even have a cot. I feel like I'm failing these kids already, and they aren't even a hundred days old.'

'This is a lot for anyone to handle, monkey,' he said. 'We've left jobs, had twins, lived with your parents and then moved across the world. Your feelings about this are normal, and they are justified, but we are not bad parents. We will laugh about this one day, I promise you.'

Two days later, we finally moved into our home in Birchgrove. It was my idea to move to the Balmain area, where Josh grew up.

Birchgrove is a beautiful Inner West neighbourhood that looks out onto Sydney Harbour and is known for its cafes, historic hotels, epic shopping strips and waterside parks. I was convinced it would be the perfect place to raise the twins. And because I was overwhelmed by all the big life changes, I loved the idea of living in an area that was familiar to Josh and one that I'd visited before.

Our house in Birchgrove quickly became my sanctuary: a gorgeous three-bedroom home with a tiny backyard and a yellow front door that we found charming. Because our belongings weren't arriving for three months, I dedicated my first couple of weeks in Sydney to turning the empty house into a family home, confident that the only thing missing from my life was a decorated house. *Once this house feels full,* I thought, *my discomfort about the move will go away.* Each day, I'd go out and purchase a new item on Josh's credit card, trying my best to bring some energy to the blank space. I was also trying my best to remain as positive as I could. But with each new day, I found myself getting sadder and sadder about the situation we found ourselves in. No bright poster or newly thrifted coffee table could bring me the joy I was searching for.

I was sad that we didn't have a textbook post-birth story of moving into our fully furnished home with our beautifully decorated nursery. Even though Josh's network was wide and willing to help, I was sad that we didn't have family around to welcome us to Sydney. I was sad that I didn't have my own friends there to support me through the transition and sad that Josh had to start working right away. He worked wild hours those first few weeks, getting up at 3.30 am to host the 6 to 10 am *Breakfast Show* on ABC Radio Sydney. That meant I needed to do the overnights solo for the first time. While he worked, I was on my own.

I often refer to those first few weeks in Sydney as my quiet period. I was now being forced to experience the rude reality of sleep deprivation, which had a major impact on me. My bubbly personality, which I'd thought would soon secure me a group of Balmain-based parenting friends, was nowhere to be seen. Even after three cups of coffee, I found it impossible to muster up the energy to talk to strangers. And even around people I knew, I felt that the light-switch dimmer on my personality had been turned low. I was tired, lonely and battling a sadness unlike any negative emotion I had experienced before. But I had kids to raise, a husband to support, and a man looking back at me in the mirror who I needed to convince that I wasn't spiralling. I needed to get out of the house for something other than a grocery shop or a walk to the park – and when I did, I could hopefully get out of my head too.

Luckily, Christmas was right around the corner: the perfect opportunity to rewrite the script with a bit of festive cheer. Christmas became my North Star. I thought of it every day throughout the first month we lived in Australia. When things were bad, I thought of decorating the Christmas trees; when things were good, I thought of Rudolph. I found ways to weave Christmas into every conversation in order to avoid talking about parenting. I needed to drown my sorrows in a cocktail of familiar holiday glee. Santa Claus was coming to town, and surely he would provide me with a cheerful bandaid to cover up the sadness that was attempting to take over my life.

Chapter Nine

The Pavlova Cry

I didn't recognise a single thing in front of me. I knew that I was standing beside a table with a selection of festive foods scattered across it, and I was familiar with most of the ingredients: mango, prawn, chilli and beetroot. But the dishes weren't … well, they weren't Christmas food – not my Christmas food, at least. And today was supposed to be Christmas.

This party was our first big event as a family since our arrival in Sydney, and it was only our fourth week in Oz, so everything was still very new to me. I was discombobulated, astonishingly taken aback by the level of culture shock I was experiencing each day. I was desperate for a slice of nostalgia, confident that it would make me feel at home even though I was thousands of miles from my family. I was longing for the comfort of Christmas food made by my mother and grandmother, but what I got was healthy beach food. I was used to warm mashed potatoes in a dark rich gravy, and turkey, cranberry sauce, stuffing, and green beans with fried onions. But instead I was looking down at ice-cold prawns, a chilled potato salad, a tray of oysters — freshly shucked by my husband, no less — and a platter of summer fruit. It was like I had landed on an alien planet, except the aliens ate Vegemite.

I was working overtime to suppress the feeling that moving to Australia was the worst decision I had ever made. This wasn't new: I'd been thinking about it for weeks.

You will not cry over a dessert, I coached myself, as tears formed in the corner of my eyes. I had been suppressing them all morning, but the strange-looking meringue mountain cake — which I would later learn was a pavlova — was sending me into hysterics. I realised I shouldn't be in public, so I dropped my empty plate on the edge of the table and made a beeline for the bathroom. The second the door slammed behind me, I fell to the floor and screamed as quietly as I possibly could.

After letting out the pavlova cry, I decided to return to the party and socially distance myself from the dessert. *Just find a comfortable spot in the back of the room,* I told myself. *You don't have to talk to people — you don't owe them that. Just stay quiet and blame it on exhaustion.*

I stood there, lifeless, nursing a champagne that had lost its fizz. Every time someone popped by to say hello, I'd give a soft smile paired with an 'I'm so tired' look. I'd make a joke about sleep deprivation being used as a form of torture, and the conversation would usually stop there. I don't blame any of those people now — everyone was just being nice. But nearly all of the interactions I had that day felt brutal. For a person in a healthy state of mind, their comments and questions would have seemed normal. But for me, it was like they all were trying to make me cry.

My siblings and I were all-American kids. We didn't eat silly food like prawns for Christmas. We ate proper things, like mashed sweet potatoes smothered in marshmallows.

'This must be such a hard transition for you.'

'How's your mum handling this? It must be so hard for her to lose her grandkids.'

One woman pushed me to the brink. 'You're so brave, don't you know that?' she offered up kindly. 'To leave your life behind like that – your job, your family, your friends. To pack it all up and move across the world. It's such a selfless act, but I just know it must be hard. Most people can't do what you're doing. Are you okay? Do you miss home? Do you miss your mum?'

I smiled as hard as I possibly could, interjecting with an endless stream of 'thank yous' and 'yeses'. But what I most wanted to say was, 'Please fucking go away.'

'Of course it's hard,' I wanted to add. 'Of course I miss home. Of course I miss my family. I just moved here a few weeks ago, so the wound is still fresh. It's Christmas, an emotional day for anyone who can't be around family. Why would you think that this line of questioning would leave someone like me in a positive state of mind?'

She walked away at some point, and it was then that I decided never to step foot in another stranger's house on Christmas Day for as long as I called Australia my home.

I began to work out an exit strategy, my eyes darting around the room, searching for my children, my bag and their toys. But what my eyes caught instead was another woman walking my way, her gaze focused directly on my face.

Abort mission, I thought. *Abort, abort, abort!*

But it was too late.

'Having fun?' she offered as she landed in front of me.

'I am,' I blatantly lied to her face.

The woman was named Jen. She was the sister-in-law of one of Josh's closest friends. She was a mother to two beautiful kids who had been expertly caring for the twins at the party. She was also a teacher. Jen was taller than me, maybe because of her high heels, with straight brown hair and a simple dress. She didn't smile much, not that I had seen, but she was smiling then.

I tried to make small talk. 'What about you? Are you having a good time?'

'So much fun,' she replied with a sarcastic tone and a cheeky eye roll.

I laughed, the first real laugh I'd had in days – maybe even weeks – which instantly put me at ease. Maybe I wouldn't need to leave. Maybe I had found someone to wallow in the misery of this holiday party with. Then she asked me if I wanted some alcohol, and I knew, instantly, that she was The One. I agreed, and watched as she scurried off to collect supplies from the kitchen.

If I'm being totally honest, I was pretty scared of Jen. I didn't know her all that well, so the judgement was unfounded. We had only met once or twice before that day, on one of my visits with Josh. She'd seemed quite serious and hadn't laughed at two of my jokes, so I'd decided that she hated me.

But here she was, approaching me with a champagne flute in each hand, clearly no hatred in sight. 'How's parenting treating you?'

'It's good. The kids are great, and Josh is a great dad. I'm having fu–'

She interrupted me. 'It doesn't have to be good. You know that, right?'

My eyes shot up from the floor to meet hers. 'Oh, yes, of course. It's just, you know, it's such a – such a – it's a gift. Gay people haven't had this opportunity for most of human history, you know? So we're – I'm good. I'm good even when it's bad.'

There was a slight pause. She was reading my face, no doubt, analysing my forced smile and watching as my eyes darted back and forth. I don't know for certain, but she had to have recognised the oh-so-familiar signs of a first-time parent in denial. She placed her hand on my shoulder, smiled and said something sweet like, 'Of course.' Then she graciously changed the subject.

For the next ten minutes or so, we traversed the boring holiday party script like veterans.

'How's work been treating you?' I asked, pretending to care.

'Oh, it's been a great year – challenging and rewarding,' she replied, playing along. She must have planned to bring the conversation back to where it had begun, because she found a non-intrusive way to check I was okay and pass down her experience. 'I'm just so impressed you're able to jungle twins. Are you getting any help?'

'Josh's friend's parents, all of them, have been super kind. But, you know, there's an age gap. I'm doing it mostly on my own at the moment.'

'I remember struggling in the beginning and keeping it all to myself. I hated it, Sean. The transition was shocking. But when I started talking openly with friends and family, being brutally honest about how hard it was and that I wasn't loving being at home, I got confirmation that I wasn't alone.'

The story she was telling wasn't mine, yet I felt as if she was describing my life. I looked into my future and imagined receiving a confirmation like that, and it seemed, maybe for the first time, like there was a glimmer of hope.

'You don't have to tell everyone,' she continued. 'A lot of people can't handle that kind of truth. But you need to find someone, one person you can be totally honest with. Someone you can look in the eye and say, "I hate this", without fear of judgement. And if you can find that, the whole experience of parenting will be better. Or it was for me, at least.'

Up until she said that, I hadn't felt like I had a right to complain. I had never seen a dad share his parenting struggles in a public forum, and the lack of any examples that would have normalised my feelings made it seem as though I shouldn't open up to those around me. I felt like a gay spy infiltrating the hetero parenting space.

I had asked for this. Actually, I'd begged for it. I hadn't needed to have kids, but I had – and now I couldn't handle it? I felt like I wasn't allowed to be unhappy.

Yet here was a mother looking me in the eye and telling me an unhappy truth that matched my experience; a friendly reminder that unhappiness doesn't discriminate.

★

I walked out of that party with a powerful new outlook on parenting thanks to Jen. We didn't become friends after that day, and I've only seen her one other time since then. But sometimes that's how it works: a friend of a friend walks into your life, maybe just for one Christmas party, and drops a lesson in your lap that entirely alters your approach.

Prior to that day, when my husband would suggest that the babies were 'acting like monsters', I would quickly shut him down: 'Don't say that! They're angels.' Now I understand he needs to vent and deserves to be heard – especially in the safety of his marriage. Shutting him down increases the likelihood he won't speak honestly with me in the future. And that, in my experience, is dangerous for all parties involved.

Prior to that day, when a friend from home would complain about how difficult her kids were being, I'd try and cheer her up in a hundred different ways, with a bit of toxic positivity to drown out the honesty. 'Awww, but they're so adorable,' I'd say. Now, I understand that what my friend really needed was to have someone validate their experience. When they chose to be honest with me, it was my responsibility to hold space for them.

Prior to that day, if I was speaking openly about my frustrations with someone and they weren't receptive to my honesty, I'd stop talking, change the subject or capitulate: 'You're right, you're right. Parenting is a blessing, I don't know why I'm complaining.' Now, I refuse to back down. I know that what's even more important than your feelings being heard is them being respected by others.

Now when I meet a new parent and sense they're presenting me with a stock-standard upbeat answer to every question, I always find a way to slip in a description of my own struggles. Then I add some version of Jen's line – 'It doesn't have to be good. You know that, right?' – into the conversation. I've done this at least twenty times in the past six years. Because maybe, just maybe, they'll hear the words coming out of my mouth and go on the exact same journey I did, paying it forward from parent to unhappy parent.

Chapter Ten

The Dirty Rubber Ball

I was at my first baby sensory class, a weekly free-play session, when it happened. Was it an accident? Surely it was – no one purposefully rolls a dirty rubber ball at full speed directly into the face of a baby. *Or maybe they do*, I thought to myself, as I decided that this woman, a complete stranger named Grace★, had just viciously attacked my helpless five-month-old son in broad daylight.

Sure, I was deliriously sleep-deprived when the incident occurred. And I hadn't properly communicated with another adult – besides my husband – in many, many days. So maybe – I said *maybe* – I was overreacting. But at that very moment, none of those details mattered: I had decided this stranger was now my archenemy. 'This villain,' I would say over the next few days, to anyone who would listen, 'has proven herself capable of performing malicious attacks on tiny humans. And that, my friends, is why I have no choice but to hold a grudge against her for the rest of our lives.'

Cooper's first baby sensory class, moments before he was assaulted by a rubber ball.

A week went by, and I had put the incident to the back of my mind. It was a non-issue, and caring for five-month-old twins in a new country with no friends while navigating cultural shock and sleep deprivation was far too mentally taxing to allow my brain to keep track of things like that – or anything that had occurred longer than a few minutes ago.

So I returned to the baby sensory class bright-eyed and bushy-tailed. Who am I kidding? I returned to the class un-showered and with a mediocre caffeine high.

The class was in the suburb of Lane Cove, at the Waterview Community Centre. When you first walked into the room, you were met with a visual display that rivalled Disneyland. Hundreds of toys, varying in size and shape, were spread across the small space. There were ball pits, slides and bubble wands. Each section of the room was designed around a theme, like the sea or the jungle. It was, for children and parents alike, a wonderland.

The class began, as it had the previous week, with a bit of forced free play. I say 'free play' even though it cost thirty-five dollars and the children were far too young to actually play. Parents arrived and unpacked their humans from tiny cars – also known as prams – before settling in at one of the four themed play stations set up around the room by our teacher, Gemma. She was young, British and genuinely positive, and she talked about parenting like it was impossible to get right. Naturally, everyone was obsessed with her.

It was our job as parents of infants, according to the official Parenting Rulebook of The World, to prioritise making small-talk with as many other parents – mostly mums, let's be real –

as possible, in hopes of one day becoming real-life friends. It's a lot like dating, except there's no anticipation of sex, and you talk exclusively about parenting. Oh, and you have a child – or two, or three – with you the entire time. Imagine your worst date ever.

Grace was unpacking her pram when I arrived. If you've lost track, she's the villain from fourteen seconds ago, keep up. She smiled at me as I walked in the room, which meant I had no choice – that is to say, under the Parenting Code of Conduct – but to park my tiny car next to her tiny car while we fumbled through an awkward five-minute conversation about sleepless nights, developmental milestones and baby-led weaning mistakes.

'Can I help you?' she asked, offering to take one of the children.

'Now that you mention it …' I said, with the energy of a professional dad-joke-giver about to nail a world-class joke. 'You don't happen to have two Xanax, a live-in nanny and a bottle of vodka, do you?'

Grace burst out laughing – one of those spit laughs that forces the individual to cover their mouth. You know, a laugh that made it clear she hadn't met a funny homosexual in the wild until now.

'But, thank you for offering,' I told her. 'If I carry both children, I don't have to get a gym membership.' I wasn't trying to continue the comedy routine – I was actually telling the truth: I considered this action to be heavy exercise and used it as the main reason why I didn't need to purchase a gym membership for the next two years.

She laughed again – it was expected by this point – as we walked towards the only available spots left on the sea-themed play mat. *This could become a friendship*, I thought as we dangled diamanté-studded bandanas over our little blobs, who wiggled like upturned turtles. *Maybe her laughter at all your jokes will make you feel better about yourself.*

She broke the silence. 'I don't know how you do it. Juggling twins? I'm barely coping with just one.'

Everyone said this – every single person I had met since having twins. Because of this, I had a Rolodex of one-liners to deploy: some that made people laugh, others that shut down the conversation immediately, and even a couple of honest responses that I would use after a few glasses of wine.

'Coffee and booze,' I said, knowing this would make her laugh again. 'But honestly, other than never sleeping and having an extremely large pram that doesn't allow me into most cafes or shops, it's such a gift to have two at the same time.'

I was lying right to her face: it turned out I hated how hard being a twin parent was. Double the nappy changes, double the feeds, double the mental breakdowns. I thought of Jen's Golden Rule, but Grace and I barely knew each other. I wasn't going to start word-vomiting my actual feelings onto her – not without a cocktail in hand. I decided to wait until our third date for that.

'True,' she said, lunging forward to grab her son, who was deep-throating a red plastic drumstick. She looked away from me when she asked, 'How has your partner handled the transition?' I could feel her emphasis on the word 'partner' tear through me, as if she was saying, 'I know your partner is a man.' It was true, but I hated that it was so obvious to others.

'*He*,' I said, 'has handled it much better than I have. He's a solid rock, picking up all the emotional pieces I keep leaving on the floor while he juggles work and my crazy ass.'

We both laughed those kinds of laughs that let each other know something isn't funny so much as brutally true. It was suddenly clear to me that we each had a story to unpack. In my case, I was genuinely concerned I might be mentally ill. I was crying multiple times a week and had recently been caught screaming, 'I hate this fucking job!' in my backyard by my next-door neighbour. But what about in her case?

'It's beautiful that he's so supportive,' she said. 'My husband is wonderful … when he's around.'

There was a long, forced pause. By 'forced', I mean that Cooper was bouncing on Stella's head, causing her to cry, so I was obligated to save my screaming daughter's life. But we also paused because we knew that 'when he's around' meant 'I'm doing everything on my own'.

'Adoption?' Grace asked.

'Surrogacy, actually,' I replied, then added my elevator pitch. 'A family member of mine donated her eggs, so we made embryos with my husband's sperm. Then, a surrogate from Minnesota carried them for us.' By that point, after enduring several rounds of questioning, I had decided that dropping the whole story in two sentences saved everyone a lot of time.

'Oh my goodness. I didn't even know that was possible!'

'Cool, right? For most of human history, this wouldn't have been possible for people like me. But because of medical advancements and selfless women, I get to be a dad. It still blows my mind.'

That was when she said it. I remember the moment so clearly because I was in the middle of blowing a raspberry above my children's faces. In retrospect, it was the very worst time to be making flatulent noises.

'He's not my son.'

I stopped my silly game, twisted my head up and stared at her, meeting her worried gaze. I was struggling to stop my eyes from bulging out of their sockets, which would have paired nicely with my internal monologue: *I'm sorry, what the literal fuck? Did you steal this child?*

I managed to respond with a calm and safe, 'Oh?' Who knew, maybe Grace was the nanny or the aunt, or maybe she was trying to make a joke about how different she and her son were in temperament and simply lacked the ability to set up a gag?

'I haven't told anyone this yet,' she said. 'No one aside from my husband, not even my sister-in-law. But something about your story just makes me feel more comfortable.'

Then, like in an annoying sitcom where someone interrupts a beautiful, season-defining moment at the exact wrong time, our teacher, Gemma, jumped in with, 'Let's begin.'

★

By the fifth class, Grace and I had a consistent routine. We'd walk in – me always later than her – and play coy. We'd sit in the same group and talk to other parents to make it seem like we weren't fully reliant on each other's presence. But because that was a hundred per cent the case, we'd then say hello to each other and shut everyone else out. 'How's he sleeping?' 'How are they eating?' 'Is your husband still working too much?' 'Is your husband still snoring?' We'd laugh and roll our eyes, commenting on how cute each other's outfits were. Then, like clockwork, we'd find our way back to the 'not my child' conversation.

After the second class had finished, I'd leant closer and lowered my voice to make it clear I was respecting her privacy. 'You said he isn't your son. What do you mean by that?'

'We couldn't conceive for years, so we finally got tested and found out it was my issue. We had to find an egg donor from Russia that kind of looked like me … and, yeah, I got pregnant shortly after that. I'm not the real bio mum.'

'Okay, got it,' I said very slowly, in hopes of buying enough time to think of something that would leave her feeling less alone. 'That's much more common than most people let on, right?'

'That's true.'

'I hope I'm not overstepping here,' I said, knowing I was definitely about to leap over the line with a pogo stick, 'but when you say "not my child", do you actually mean it?'

'I mean, no. No, no, no. Kind of. I guess I'm struggling a bit with that.'

'But you carried him, right? And birthed him?'

'That's right,' she replied sheepishly.

'I've seen you breastfeed him halfway through class. And even if you didn't do any of those things, you're raising him – like, every single day. Taking him to this silly class. Talking to me. No one else is doing all that. You *are* the mother. He *is* your son.'

She stared at the floor, nodding repeatedly as if trying to convince herself that it was all true. 'I know you're right. It's just harder some days than others to remember that. I wanted to be a mum so bad and then it took a different path than I expected. All these mums just seem so connected to their children, and I don't know if that's why I'm not. Then I saw you being so confident about your role in their lives – even though they aren't ... well, they are, but they aren't. Sorry, I just thought maybe you'd understand.'

'I do.' I reached out, and she took my hand.

Right there, in that community centre nestled in the hills of Lane Cove at 9.58 on a rainy Monday morning, Grace started to cry.

★

Grace wasn't the first or the last parent I met who felt their relationship to their child wasn't 'real enough', either for themselves or for society. Something about my gayness and the obvious hurdles Josh and I had needed to jump over to make our family a reality meant that I was a magnet for people looking to vent about their unique path to parenthood.

There was Raquel★ a mum I met once at a playground in Balmain. She'd adopted two girls with her exact skin tone, so she really struggled when people said, 'They look just like their mother.'

Kate★, a gorgeous young mother I met once at a local library, had recently taken custody of her late sister's child. 'When does aunting end and mothering begin?' she shared after reprimanding her kids.

Then there was Kev★ from a cafe, and Abbie★ from a yoga studio, and Shelby★ from my Instagram DMs.

All of these parents were strangers, each with their own journey — surrogacy, IVF, adoption, remarriage — but they all had one thing in common. I could hear it in their voices, see it in their eyes: it was shame. Their version of parenting wasn't what they had imagined, and at some level they thought it wasn't good enough or normal enough, and whatever script they'd been force-fed by society all their lives confirmed their experience wasn't valid.

But I didn't feel that way, not since becoming a father to Stella and Cooper. You earn the role of being a parent. You put in the work. You do the late nights and the nappy changes. You make the food and buy the clothes and teach them about consent. DNA only gets you so far — the starting line, really. It's the amount of love you give that earns you your parenting title.

Chapter Eleven

The Dictator

Although they gave birth to my husband, I didn't know them very well. Josh and I had been together for six years, but because we were living in America and then Australia, while his parents, Mary Ann and Henri, were in Hastings, England, my opportunities for getting to know them better were few and far between. We had celebrated Christmases, video-chatted each month, and even gone on a few holidays together, but the travel windows were short, and I was always on my best behaviour. That is to say, they had never met the real Sean: their always anxious, can't-stop-talking, sometimes catty and always crude son-in-law. I wasn't sure if we really understood the reality of each other – not yet, at least. So when they got off the plane from London and settled into their apartment in Leichhardt, a fifteen-minute drive from Birchgrove, I was nervous.

I had great expectations that my in-laws would swoop in and fix all of my problems. The twins were five months old, and I still hadn't made any genuine friends in Sydney. I had a few strong connections, but none who had made it past the 'we periodically talk at the playground' phase. I spent ninety per cent of my time alone with the twins and had fallen, unfortunately, into a habit of lying to most of my family and friends about my experience of living in Sydney. Mostly this was out of fear of hearing 'I told you so' or worrying them about my mental health struggles. However, if all went according to plan, Mary Ann and Henri would instantly become part of my tribe. I could properly vent to them about my parenting struggles, and they already understood the painful realities of moving to a new country: Mary Ann from New Zealand and Henri from Switzerland. Most importantly, they would feel a pull to assist us in watching the twins. Which meant that I'd finally get a chance to exercise or, I dunno, sleep. I was more exhausted than I thought was safe for someone taking care of tiny humans.

Mary Ann had been surrounded by strong-willed men for most of her adult life, raising two spirited boys after marrying a brilliant, pugnacious man. Back before we knew the sex of the twins, it had seemed she might spend the rest of her days as a matriarch to a brood of boys. The last time I'd seen her, I hadn't been shocked when she'd jokingly whispered, 'Bring a granddaughter.' Now I had that precious little girl in my hands, and I was about to hand her over to her grandmother.

The first meeting in their Leichhardt apartment was everything I wanted it to be. When we arrived, Mary Ann had cleared a space at the centre of the living room for the twins to play in, sandwiched on either side by a couch and two armchairs. While the children squirmed around on the floor, the adults sat nearby and caught up for hours, having a real, adult conversation.

If Josh is my Prince Charming, then meet the Queen and King: Mary Ann and Henri.

First, we spoke about the twins, updating their grandparents on their evolving personalities and recent developmental milestones. Stella was tough, Cooper was timid. Cooper giggled easily and Stella made you work for it. Stella and Cooper had striking dark brown eyes that were beginning to pop through the grey haze. Stella had developed a new habit of reaching for the brown fluff atop Cooper's head and pulling it. Cooper had a lazy eye when he was tired that we were going to see a specialist about, and Stella was already rolling over on both sides.

As we ate lunch, we graduated to more exciting topics. We talked about Trump's first year in the White House and the investigation into Russian interference in the US election. We talked about global warming, high temperatures in Australia, and hurricanes in the Americas. We talked about Harvey Weinstein, the #MeToo movement and gender inequality in the workforce. We talked about Josh's new job at ABC Radio Sydney, my inability to make new friends, and how parenting had changed since Mary Ann and Henri raised their boys. For the first time in many months, I found myself using my adult brain with people who weren't my husband. I relished the chance to leave parenting behind, even if just for an hour, and talk about the world. When you have babies in a pram beside you or strapped to your tummy in a carrier, parenting is the only thing people want to talk to you about, and I wanted to talk about, well, anything else.

A spark lit up inside of me, bringing tears to my eyes. 'I needed this – we needed this,' I said as the emotions overcame me.

Henri stood up, walked over to my side and asked if he could give me a hug. As I eagerly accepted his embrace, I felt as if my fantasies about this meeting – of becoming a formidable crew who could gladly chat for hours while we watched over the twins – had come true.

I had so many stories I wanted to share, parenting issues I had experienced that I wanted to word-vomit into safe hands, and I knew that Mary Ann would be a perfect listener. Everyone who was close to her – each one of her friends and family members – waxed poetic about her warm, motherly nature and powerful empathy. I knew that if anyone could support me through these sticky situations, it was her.

When there was a lull in the conversation, I opened up about a recent encounter. 'A stranger asked me last week if I was the twins' uncle.'

'They said *what*?' asked Henri.

'What do you think prompted that?' Mary Ann added.

I explained that this had been the third or fourth time it had happened since our move to Oz. The first time, I'd thought nothing of it – you know, a harmless mistake. But after the second and third times, I'd detected a trend and decided to dig a bit deeper.

'I thought it was because I'm young,' I told the group, while Josh topped up my drink. 'Or maybe because I was really engaged with the kids in their pram, a potential outlier in a sea of less playful fathers. But the more I think about it, the more I believe something else might be at play.'

Mary Ann and Henri were leaning forward and looking very engaged. I felt as though I was talking to my own parents, so I gave in and explored my theory with them without fear of sounding like an anxious brat.

To paint a clearer picture for them, I shared the most recent example of this phenomenon. I was waiting for a coffee outside the front door of our favourite cafe. The twins were sleeping, so I wasn't speaking to them. I was just texting, wearing a green shirt that read *DANCE* and very short shorts. I had strappy Greek-style sandals on, and a collection of gold bracelets that I'd found at a local op shop.

'Are you their uncle?' the barista asked out of thin air.

'Nope, I'm their dad,' I replied without hesitation.

'That's nice.'

It wasn't a rude exchange – short and sweet, really. The moment went by as fast as it had come. She made the assumption, I corrected her, then she responded politely before handing over my coffee. It wasn't awkward, not for her. But my palms were beginning to sweat.

'To most people,' I said to my in-laws, 'her question might have seemed harmless. She was just being friendly, right? How could she possibly know I'm their father? But on the other hand, how could she possibly know I'm their uncle?'

Mary Ann jumped in. 'Oh, sweetie, it's true that very few men with children would randomly be lumped into the role of uncle.'

'Right? I'm only making a big deal out of it because it feels quite strange. "Nanny", I could totally understand. "Older brother" as a flirtatious acknowledgement of my youthful glow? Sure. But "uncle"? Why the hell "uncle"?'

'Yes, why the hell "uncle"?' said Henri.

'To me, it's clear what she meant. She asked if I was the uncle because she could tell that I was gay. She watched me as I strutted into that venue. She listened as my slightly flamboyant voice pierced through the sombre morning energy of the empty cafe. And because her deductive reasoning concluded that I was, in fact, a homosexual, it meant that the twins couldn't possibly be mine – because gay people don't have kids.'

I was pouring my heart out onto the floor. That barista's question had left a mark. I told them it had felt like a straight slap across my gay face. I explained that the transaction – the fourth of many homophobic assumptions I would have to encounter on my parenting journey – had stuck with me for days.

'Oh, Sean,' Mary Ann said softly. 'This is such a unique situation, isn't it?'

'I just want to be seen as a father,' I said.

'You are! You know this, and now she knows this. But I do wonder how much of it goes deeper than the exchange?'

I looked Mary Ann in the eye, waiting for her to elaborate. I was hoping she might give me an answer, solving all my problems. But she didn't. She just tilted her head and looked at me with a warm smile.

'I guess I'm mad at Sydney a bit. I expected more, like the city would be further evolved than it actually is – not just Sydney, but the world. In my mind, we're everywhere. Gay families are visible. We adopt, we have kids. But clearly, there's a lot more work to do.'

'And you and Josh are the perfect people to help with that.'

I knew it wasn't the fault of these random strangers: they just hadn't been given the opportunity to learn more about us yet. That waitress was used to seeing a certain type of dad walk into her cafe, while I sat outside that norm. If I wanted to choose to get upset about the situation and never wear short-shorts or bracelets again, then I totally could. Or I could use the frustration as fuel to make the world a better place for the next generation of queer parents.

'Thank you for that,' I told Mary Ann. 'That was really useful.'

'You're welcome, my dear. It's been very exciting to be welcomed into your life.'

'We should be thanking you,' Henri added with a fatherly wink.

This was it. This was what my future looked like: warm dialogue with smart people over a cheeky cocktail.

★

We took a break from chatting while Mary Ann and Josh moved into the bedroom to feed and settle Stella. Henri and I remained in the living room, the sun starting to pour in through the French doors that were opened out onto the balcony. I was sitting on the floor, my legs tightly bound in a pretzel position as I attempted to crack the sleep deprivation out of my body. Henri was pottering about, while I supervised Cooper during his tummy time.

My father-in-law paused to bask in the glory of the sublime cumulus clouds that were quickly moving past. 'Humour me for a second, will you?' he said, motioning me onto the balcony.

'Of course.' I moved Cooper on to his back, climbed off the floor and went out through the doorway.

'Look at that sky. Look at it. That–' he paused '–is God.'

I wasn't sure if he was serious. I knew he was a proud Jewish man, and he often dropped Yiddish slang into our conversations, but the topic of religion hadn't come up in our earlier meetings. I didn't know if he knew that I was raised Roman Catholic, but it didn't really matter. The collection of clouds above us, changing colour every second like a kaleidoscope, was a deity I was more than willing to get behind.

'In your old age you start to appreciate nature,' he said. 'When you have the time to just stop and stare at it, you do. And when you do, you realise what you've been missing.'

He was right. Just then, as if on cue, Cooper started crying and I scurried inside, leaving Henri to admire God's painting in peace.

I felt a deep connection with Henri from the moment I met him. Witty and charming, he was a professional actor well known for his role in one of Australia's most beloved sitcoms, *Mother and Son*, in the 80s and 90s. After a young adulthood performing in musicals, taking vocal lessons, studying theatre at college, moving to New York City to make it big and then walking away from the industry when I couldn't handle the instability, I was in total awe that Henri had successfully navigated a career in the arts for fifty years.

When he spoke, especially about theatre, I always shut up and listened. Every chance I got, I'd pick his brain about acting. I asked him about his approach to auditioning, his character development process, and how it felt to be a straight actor cast in the groundbreaking gay play, *Boys in the Band*, in the late 60s. You can take the boy out of the theatre, but you'll never take the theatre out of the boy. When most of the world seemed to ignore my relationship to the arts – I mean, I *had* quit – Henri refused to do so.

'How long did you tap, give or take?' he'd asked me over lunch that day.

'I started when I was five and stopped when I was twenty-two.'

'Then you're a hoofer! It's in your bones. No one can take that away from you – no one.'

Henri gave me permission to acknowledge and talk confidently about a past I was proud of. Over time, he also gave me permission to believe that I might want to make another attempt at a career in the arts – that I might take the lessons learned in our conversations about his career and apply them to my own. Because performing is, like he said, in my bones.

Henri returned to the living room and stood next to me as I rocked Cooper with my right foot in a baby bouncing chair Josh and I brought everywhere we went. My father-in-law stared down at Cooper, who was drifting off to sleep, and whispered under his breath, 'Hitler failed.'

He kept his focus on Cooper, but I turned to look up at him, soaking in his words.

He was grinning from ear to ear, shaking his head from left to right. His gaze joined mine. 'Do you know what I mean?'

'I do. Well, I think I do.'

'Another generation of Jews born into this world, despite it all.'

I couldn't think of a verbal response that was worthy of such a moment. I just stood up, hugged my father-in-law tight, and laughed through the tears streaming down my face.

I had badly needed a reminder that this job, this opportunity to parent Stella and Cooper, was so much bigger than me. Since their birth, I'd become so lost in a monotonous loop of 'Am I doing good enough?' and 'What am I going to do next?' that I had forgotten about everything – and everyone – who had come before me. Sleep deprivation and pure adrenaline had ripped away my ability to consider what it had really taken for Josh and I to get here.

I felt small, but in the very best of ways. It was as though I had stepped out of the story of my own singular life and fallen into the pages of a much longer tale about our two families.

This child sleeping in front of me was alive because of our ancestors. On one side, Holocaust survivors who had fled the Nazis to create a better life for their children. On the other, Cuban refugees who had smuggled themselves into the cargo hold of a plane to escape Fidel Castro after he took their homes and businesses. My five-month-old twins were an extension of that story. Our ancestors had fought and persevered for them, and they were living proof it had all been worth it. Communism and fascism had failed so that children like Cooper and Stella could thrive.

Ever since that conversation with my father-in-law, I tell anyone who will listen the story of how Hitler made me a better dad.

Chapter Twelve

The Silent Night

The bellowing of our two children couldn't wake Josh from his slumber. I lay there in silence next to him, wondering if it was him or me. Was he too deep of a sleeper, or was I too light? Was he too careless, or was I too anxious? If it weren't for me, I had convinced myself, the twins probably would have been abducted by a dingo by now. Surely he'd wake up at some point. In four minutes? Six minutes? Eleven minutes into this epic twin opera? But he wouldn't, not without me elbowing him first. So I'd give in for the sixth or seventh time that night and drag myself across the hallway.

It was pitch-black in both rooms, theirs and ours, but I navigated the obstacle course like a ninja with expert night vision. I had memorised the exact amount of steps I could take from the edge of my bed to the lip of the door before I'd smash my foot and blame my husband.

The second I entered their room, the delicate resettling

routine would begin. Seven months into parenting, I had mastered it, never deviating from the script.

'Dada's here,' I'd say. 'I'm here now, don't you worry. Everything is going to be okay.'

I'd plop myself on the floor between their cots, sitting cross-legged as I stretched out my arms to search for their dummies. We always left two or three around their heads at night, a trick Josh had picked up from a close friend, so I was destined to find one quickly. I'd plug each child up and break into a soft performance of 'Silent Night', my go-to lullaby. I'd remain in the room, stroking their bellies, until I was certain they were asleep.

I would then push my way backwards down the rug, slowing the tempo of the song, standing up just before the wooden floorboards began, then tiptoeing to my bed, avoiding the creaky spots. The second my head hit the pillow, I'd fall asleep as if nothing had happened.

One night I was there, back at the scene of the crime, in the same position I'd sat in every single night for the past five months. But this night, I found myself there for the tenth time in a row. Something was off. The dummies couldn't be found, the lullabies were ineffective and the lingering smell of baby shit — a special bouquet of faecal odours — wafted around the room. Mary Ann and Henri had been very helpful since their arrival in Sydney, just as I'd hoped, but they couldn't magically cure the twins of their sleep issues.

My patience was waning. I made my way through the dark house with my hand running along the wall, down the hallway, through the living room, around our record-player and into the kitchen, where I held open the refrigerator with my elbow for light as I mixed and then microwaved some baby formula.

I stubbed my toe at the entrance of their bedroom, an amateur move. I was afraid their cries might wake their father, whose alarm would be going off at 3.30 am, so I was working much faster than I usually would. I picked both babies up, cradling one in each arm, and dropped to the floor beside their crib. To my right, Cooper was wailing as he refused to drink the formula, while to my left, Stella spat her dummy out and joined in.

It was then that I felt it: a warm and wet puddle of poop forming on my left arm.

I knew what needed to be done, but the balancing act of grabbing new nappies and clothes and keeping two bottles inside of two children's mouths, all while attempting to keep our small house quiet, seemed an impossible feat.

This was my tipping point. I'd officially had it.

I picked up Stella first, shit dripping from her back, and dropped her into her crib. I repeated this careless manoeuvre with Cooper, who had finished his bottle and promptly passed out. Then I exited the room, Stella's faint cries behind me, and slammed their door.

I went into our bedroom to greet my sleeping husband. 'I'm fucking out of here!' I screamed at Josh. 'They're *your* responsibility now.'

He shook awake, but before he could respond, I was gone.

I slammed our bedroom door loud enough to wake the neighbours. After grabbing my phone and a set of keys, I stormed out the front door. It was 1 am and the only light came from a faint streetlamp across from our home. There was silence in Birchgrove that morning, but the angry soundtrack in my mind was screeching as I turned on the car. I threw my phone against the magnetic holder on the dashboard, typed *Sydney International Airport* into my GPS, then manically drove towards the highway.

At the back of my mind, in my worst moments, the plan had been coalescing for a while. I would escape to Mexico. I wanted nothing to do with the twins or Josh ever again, and I refused to let my mother know that I wasn't a good parent. I had a good enough understanding of Spanish, having grown up around so many Cubans, so I decided that hiding in a small Mexican town wouldn't be too difficult. There, I'd change my name and become a sex worker. I hated my husband for dragging me to Australia, I hated my children for ruining my perfect life, and I hated that I couldn't make any friends in Sydney. But above all else, I hated myself. This was all my fault. How had I let this happen?

Mom had given me an amazing example to follow, a template that seemed foolproof for a life of happiness. I had tried to replicate her success, but somewhere along the way I'd decided that I had failed miserably. My total exhaustion meant I was always angry at my helpless infants. Mary Ann and Henri were taking the twins once, sometimes twice a week for a few hours, but that didn't help with my night-time routine. I just couldn't get them to sleep and I couldn't get them to eat enough … and did I mention that I couldn't get them to sleep? Terrible days bled into terrible weeks. After months of waiting for it all to get better, hoping that baby sensory class or a fully furnished home or my in-laws would miraculously change everything and that my sadness would lift, I decided there wasn't a light at the end of the tunnel.

I drove straight to the airport, a twenty-minute trip without traffic, and parked with the hazards on. There was no one around aside from an employee smoking a cigarette. For some reason, I couldn't get myself to turn off the car. I was running away, so what would I do with the keys? But I flung open the door and put my right foot on the ground. 'Just one more step,' I said out loud. 'One more step, and this nightmare is fucking over.'

That was when I realised my brain was broken.

I had tried to hide it, brushing the signs of severe depression under the dirty IKEA rug on our living-room floor for months. But as I sat there at the airport, my right foot on the pavement of a childless and husbandless future, one without any family members or old friends, and my left foot trapped in a reality that I hated, I knew I needed serious help.

I put my right foot back in the car, closed the door and drove back home to Birchgrove.

*

I had a long and tumultuous history with mental health issues, but until now they had never gotten this bad. I had never worked out an exit strategy, never researched the best places to disappear to, never considered walking away from a life that I once wanted. I didn't care who would be sad after I left, and that really scared me. I didn't care that my children would grow up without one of their dads. I didn't even care that my loving husband would have to do it all on his own. *He'll find another man, a stable and sane partner in crime – he's better off without me,* I'd tell myself in the shower, the sound of the water muffling my cries. I just couldn't think past my sadness anymore, as though a miserable narrator had taken over the script inside my mind: *My life is terrible, my children are horrible and my husband is a monster who can't hear them crying at night. I need to run away or kill myself.*

After I returned from the airport, I quietly tucked myself back into bed as if nothing had happened. As I lay there, slowly drifting off to sleep, I felt riddled with embarrassment. The thought of telling anyone made me feel sick to my stomach. I wasn't sure if I would ever tell a soul – not even my husband – what had transpired. I remember thinking, *The Great Mexican Escape is a secret you'll carry to your grave.* I woke up the next morning and explained to Josh over our morning coffee that I needed to be checked into a mental health hospital. He could tell from the tone of my voice that I wasn't joking, so he immediately booked me in to see our GP, without having to ask. 'We'll get you some help,' he whispered in my ear, as I sobbed into his shoulder in our kitchen. 'You don't have to do this on your own. I'm right here with you.'

I couldn't respond to him, finding it impossible to speak. The weight of the situation and its severity had caused me to go mute. But I thought, *I really fucking hope he's right.*

When I arrived at our local medical clinic two days later, the children at home with Josh, I was in a state of shock. I was embarrassed about what had occurred and afraid of what the GP and Josh might say when I told them the truth. Like an addict arriving at rehab, or so I imagined, I felt like this was the beginning of the end. But what would the end look like? All these months I hadn't spoken out loud about how I was really feeling, not even to my own husband. I'd been doing my best to mask the dark reality, partly in fear of having the kids taken away from me. But after my airport visit, I knew that I needed some help, and I wasn't leaving that office until I got it.

'How are you feeling today, Sean?' the doctor asked, the second my butt hit the seat in front of him.

I had become an expert at faking happiness, leveraging every ounce of my college-level acting training to force Oscar-worthy smiles. But I was now so deep in a hole of despair that my ability to care about what others thought of me was non-existent, so I skipped the pleasantries. 'I'm really not good.'

'Can you tell me more about it?' he asked.

I dove right in. 'I've been really struggling for the past few weeks, maybe months. I'm just emotionally not in a good place, and I think – and my husband thinks – that I might need to get some help. I'm sad all of the time, I'm angry at my husband and at my kids, and I've started to think that maybe it would be better if I just wasn't here anymore.'

My GP, a spritely man in his fifties who reminded me a lot of my father, looked me in the eye and said, 'Let's get you some help then.' He went over to his computer and began to type. He asked me a series of questions about what I was struggling with, and I did my best to be brutally honest while staring at the floor in shame. As he spoke, the printer ejected a form with orange writing at the top: *The Edinburgh Postnatal Depression Scale.* 'This is mostly given to women. But some fathers do struggle emotionally after the birth of their children, and I think it would be smart to complete this form while you're here.'

He presented me with ten simple scenarios about how I'd been feeling over the past seven days, each with four answers ranging from 'Yes, most of the time' to 'No, not at all'.

Have I been able to laugh? No, not at all.

Have I looked forward with enjoyment to things? No, not at all.

Have I blamed myself unnecessarily?

Have I been anxious? Scared? Unhappy? Sad?

Have I struggled with sleeping?

Have I been crying?

And lastly, *Have I thought about harming myself?*

Nearly all of my answers fell into the 'extreme' category.

It wasn't until I was responding honestly to questions from my doctor that I realised my situation might be even worse than I had imagined. I knew I was sad, I knew I was tired, and I was afraid of what had transpired at the airport, but was my mental health potentially endangering my children?

My GP tallied up the score and wrote a double-digit number that began with a 2 at the top of the page. I didn't know what it meant, but I would later learn that anything above a 13 is grounds for referring the patient to a psychiatrist or psychologist as the 'likelihood of depression is high'. My GP looked up from the page and gave me one of those smiles everyone recognises as saying, 'This isn't good, but you're in the right place.'

Josh had suggested that, no matter the outcome of my appointment, I should speak to our doctor about attending Tresillian. As Australia's largest not-for-profit child and family health organisation, it provided expert advice and assistance to families – mostly mothers – during the early months after birth. Josh had spoken on the phone to a previous patient, who had explained that Tresillian was well known nationally for assisting first-time parents in mastering the process of resettling a baby back to sleep.

I flagged the idea shortly after taking the Edinburgh test, and my GP agreed that because sleep deprivation was likely the cause of a lot of my struggles, attempting to get on the list for Tresillian was a strong option. He said that while it was difficult to get a bed at one of the four nearby locations, my postnatal depression diagnosis would mean I'd be placed at the top of the waitlist. He explained that I would meet with psychologists, psychiatrists and nurses while I was there, and that depending on my progress I could extend my visit for a few days. In his experience, nearly every patient benefited in some way from their support, and he was hopeful it would give me an opportunity to catch up on sleep and get some professional assistance with the children. 'When you're well rested and back home, we can have a conversation about an ongoing mental health treatment plan.'

I didn't feel any better as I left his office, not in any measurable emotional way, but I was relieved that something – anything – was happening. There was no magic pill to make me feel better, but at least there was a diagnosis and a plan. I wasn't 'crazy': I was depressed. I wasn't a terrible monster: I was exhausted and struggling in silence.

Yet as I walked home from the clinic, I still felt embarrassed. This was the worst-case scenario my mom had been trying to help me avoid. She'd questioned me in hopes of preparing me for the difficult road ahead. She couldn't have predicted it would get this bad, but I thought, *She was right.*

At home I updated Josh on what our doctor had shared. I sat on the couch holding Stella in my arms, and I whispered, 'I'll do better', over and over again, hoping this manta would somehow find its way into her brain to make up for all my failed attempts at soothing her.

Josh contacted the four Tresillian locations near our home, but it would be two weeks before a spot opened up at one of them. When things got bad as I waited, and they definitely did, I had Tresillian as my North Star. Josh stepped up over that fortnight, taking time off work and giving me space. Every time I was alone or taking charge of the night routine, I would remind myself that I had a team waiting to help me, and that actually helped – the knowledge I wasn't in this alone anymore made things a bit better.

Before I knew it, Josh and I were packing the car for our 'holiday' at the Tresillian Family Care Centre in Nepean, an hour's drive from our house.

★

When we pulled into the parking lot outside of the centre, I was overwhelmed by shame. My husband, who had a calm but concerned look on his face, was stroking my knee. He was dressed for work and here he was having to drop his broken husband and tiny twins off to get help at a centre for adults who couldn't handle the responsibilities of parenthood. I learned later that Josh was going through his own catastrophe of stress and anxiety, but at the time all I could focus on was myself. For whatever reason, Josh didn't need this kind of help: only I did. And that made me feel like shit. Shit for him, because his husband, who had promised he would be a natural at this whole fatherhood thing, was failing miserably. And shit for me, because I was the one failing.

As we walked towards the front entrance, we passed a family who were leaving. The mother looked as if she was returning from war, her eyes sunken like a racoon's and her clothes in disarray. Her husband, a short man with ginger hair, a large brown beard and an oversized business suit, was carrying their baby in a car seat and walking two steps behind the woman. He looked ashamed, his head dropped low, not even glancing in our direction. I will never know for sure, but I imagined that he was hoping we didn't know each other from 'the outside world' – that he was, much like me, embarrassed to have found himself there.

When Josh and I got to the front door, we were greeted by a smiling young nurse who said she was expecting us. She assisted us in filling out the arrival paperwork and then walking us down the hallway to our hospital-style bedroom. Josh would leave for work each day and return most nights, but I would remain there with the twins until further notice. As we walked down that hallway, women were sitting outside their rooms with defeat on their faces. Each of them looked me up and down, then averted her gaze as I glanced at her. Embarrassment, it seemed, was the theme of the day.

My first thought while settling in was, *There's not a single man in here.* There were just a few dropping off and picking up. This sent me down an emotional spiral. When my husband left for work, I closed the door to the room, placed the twins down for a nap in their cots, shut myself in the bathroom, sat in the dry tub and cried. *Men*, I thought, *aren't supposed to be in here.* Men, straight men, would never find themselves in a facility like this. This was a place for women, who understandably needed help. They'd just permanently altered their bodies during pregnancy and childbirth, then a lot of them had started breastfeeding. Many of them were putting their careers on hold. As well as juggling post-birth physical and hormonal transformations, they were all taking a leadership role in keeping their tiny humans alive. But me, I hadn't been pregnant. I wasn't dealing with postpartum physical changes. I didn't have to breastfeed eight to twelve times a day. No, I just needed to keep my tiny humans alive, and I couldn't even do that. Should I have given myself some slack? Absolutely. But I simply wasn't capable of thinking positively.

The emotional start to my week-long stay wasn't a great introduction to the centre's potential. But over the course of my time there, I gained some valuable insights.

For years, my Instagram feed had been crowded with parents who seemed to enjoy every single second of the parenting journey. Online, I never once saw another parent crying or failing – not back then, at least – and this left me feeling like a failure in a sea of success cases. But at Tresillian, I was surrounded by all these women who were struggling too. We didn't need to pretend: we were there because we needed help, and we knew that about each other. Whenever one of us opened up about a seemingly unique issue, during a late-night snack break or

I took this photo of the twins – Cooper (left) and Stella (right) – shortly after
checking into Tresillian. I uploaded it to Instagram and pretended I wasn't in
the middle of a mental breakdown.

a walk around the facilities, the others almost always spoke of experiencing it too, so we'd wallow in suffering together. I felt more and more like I wasn't the only failure on the planet – I was just another parent in a long line of parents who found the early days with a baby or two unbearably difficult.

I left Tresillian feeling hopeful. But I also left wondering how many other parents – especially men – were suffering in silence and just weren't talking about it.

*

It was at Tresillian that one of the many doctors I met with suggested I go on an antidepressant. That was the trigger for putting together a mental health plan with my GP when I returned home. At first I was adamantly against it, having struggled with mental health medication in the past and feeling mortified that things had come to this, but my doctor convinced me when he said, 'We'll just use the medicine for a short period of time to get the old Sean back.' He added, 'If we can get your sleep, appetite and mood regulated, then your interest in daily living will change too. And once we get your rational brain back, it will become easier for you to deal with many of the parenting issues you're faced with.'

With the help of a psychologist I met with weekly, we agreed I would begin on a small dose of sertraline, sold under the brand-name Zoloft. This would hopefully lift me out of the deep fog I'd been lost in since moving to Australia.

I needed a window of time where it didn't matter if I was out of it for a few days, so we agreed to wait to start the medicine until I was home with my family in New Hampshire a few weeks later. It was a trip that Josh had planned before we even left for Australia so that everyone – my mom especially – had a specific reunion date to look forward to.

I FaceTimed my mom and cautiously explained the situation to her: 'I haven't wanted to tell you this out of fear of scaring you, but I've been really struggling the last few months. I went to the doctor recently and was diagnosed with postnatal depression. Now, I need to go on meds.'

'Oh, Seanie.' She placed her hand over her mouth and then down to her heart. 'You never have to keep anything from me. I'm sorry you've been hurting and that you felt you couldn't share it with us. I would have dropped everything and flown out to help you immediately. I will always fly to help you.'

'Thank you, Mom. I know.' I was crying. 'I'm just happy I'm coming back home.'

When we arrived in New Hampshire, I handed over the twins to the safe embrace of both my parents. With my sister there for support, my brother and sister-in-law visiting nightly, and Josh by my side, I safely took a few days to transition on to the meds. I mostly sat in an armchair in the living room, staring out at the lake beside the house, my happy place. By the second day, I could feel parts of my brain rewiring. I was lethargic but incredibly happy, desperate for further mental respite. When Josh asked how I was feeling, I said, 'Like I'm stoned. It's really great.'

A few months later, I found myself back at the scene of the crime. My husband sleeping, yet again, in the bedroom across the hall. And there I was, yet again, very, very tired. Tresillian had given me many gifts, but it wasn't the miracle worker that many bloggers had claimed it to be. Josh and I still struggled getting the twins to sleep, and I still wasn't sleeping well myself. But something had changed for the better: the old Sean, the one capable of rational thinking, was there. He had taken back the narrator role.

I sat with my arms on my children's backs as I sang 'Silent Night' and I realised another difference was my new-found pride in myself. I had done it – powered through one of the most emotionally and physically draining times of my entire life. It was touch and go for a minute there, but I hadn't run away to Mexico or taken my life.

Our struggles were far from over. The children were still young, and I had many obstacles ahead. I had dealt with depression before, and I would likely deal with it again, but I wasn't suffocating in silence any longer. I had raised my hand, asked for help, accepted the offer of support and done the work necessary to begin tackling my mental health. I wasn't embarrassed anymore about going to Tresillian, or ashamed that I felt like a solitary depressed man lost in a woman's parenting world. And I wasn't ashamed to admit that I was on medication or that I couldn't manage sleep training without support. I was on the right path, and that was worth celebrating. I sang the final word of 'Silent Night' and reached over to pat myself on the back.

Now when people ask if it was hard for me to raise twins, I tell them the bloody truth. I tell them the story of Mexico and Tresillian, and the small dose of Zoloft that saved my life.

Chapter Thirteen

The Ladies

I had been watching them from afar for months, slowly mapping out my plan of attack. My thirst for friendship in Australia had turned me into a creepy spy committed to finagling his way into a local mothers' group.

In my pre-parenting life, I had never struggled making friends, especially with women. As a confident gay man, I was used to getting their attention. My sass and wit were usually an easy sell, along with the involuntary stream of compliments that seemed to pour from my mouth. But for whatever reason, local Australian mums completely ignored me.

At first, I thought it was because I was a man. I saw fathers around, of course, but that was almost exclusively on the weekends. During weekdays, the playgrounds and cafes were packed with mothers and children. I imagined that after a lifetime of being cautious around men, the mums were considerably more wary of me than they were of each other.

I then decided it was because of my age. Most of the other mothers, especially in the Balmain area, were in their late thirties to early forties. I was twenty-nine, but had recently lost some weight and looked prepubescent.

Whatever the reason, I wasn't making any friends. I tried starting conversations by complimenting outfits and helping children when they fell. I even put my cards on the table and found ways to drop 'I just moved here from America' feelers into any conversation. But the ladies simply weren't picking up what I was putting down.

Josh suggested that I call the nearest hospital to see if they might assign me to a local parenting group. When we took our antenatal classes together in Los Angeles many months prior, the organisers connected the participants and suggested we start a WhatsApp group. Josh and I never joined because we planned on living in a different country by the time the babies were born, but it gave me confidence when I found out that the system was the same in Oz. Unfortunately, when I called, I was connected to a very confused and abrupt receptionist.

'You're about to be a dad?' she said.

'No, I already have twins who are a few months old,' I replied.

'But your twins were born here?' she asked.

'No, sorry. They were born abroad.'

'I'm not sure how to help you. We work with parents whose children were born in this hospital,' she said sharply, as if she wanted to rush me off the phone. 'Go to nsw.gov.au and find the Family and Relationships tab. You might be able to find a group there.'

I navigated my way through the government website but struggled to find a group that made sense for me, feeling alienated by the 'Mothers' Group' label (they have since added Fathers' and Parenting Groups). I googled 'Local Balmain Parenting Group' shortly after and was again left feeling discouraged when the top search result was 'Inner West Mums', a Facebook group that required you to be accepted by an administrator. I applied, thinking that they might sense the gayness through my profile picture and let my gender slide, but I'm still waiting for them to accept my request.

It was then that I decided to give up. I often think back to that time in my life and wonder why I didn't try harder. I knew what a difference a friendship group would have made for my mental health, but I lacked the necessary grit and dedication to make it a reality. It embarrasses me now, but I just wanted it all handed to me. I thought, naively, that new parents – no matter their gender, sexuality or nationality – would simply be contacted by the Australian government and given all the necessary tools needed to thrive. But the government never called, and I resented having to figure it out on my own. I wanted friends, but like a millennial who stubbornly refuses to sign up for online dating, I wanted it to happen in person. Like the olden days.

Then, I found them: four ladies who met twice a week, Tuesday and Thursday, at the Mort Bay Park playground with one child each. The mums ranged in age from their early thirties to mid-forties, but it appeared that their kids were the same age – which looked from afar to be the very same age as Stella and Cooper.

The Ladies

I called these women the 'Sexless in the City Ladies' behind their backs, partly because their hair colours matched those of the iconic *Sex and the City* quartet: Charlotte, Miranda, Carrie and Samantha. But mostly because I overheard them laughing about never having sex again. I quickly learned, when they offered up the information to an older woman passing by, that they were a local mothers' group who had met through their hospital. They were funny and fashionable, and I decided to make them my friends.

Charlotte★ was British, and she seemed like the leader of their group. She was the most organised – well, the most anal – always arriving the earliest with a picnic blanket and a tower of Tupperware packed full of mother-friendly nibbles. From a fashion perspective, she fit the Charlotte description perfectly: she loved a Chanel-inspired tweed look, gelled her hair back into a tight ponytail and wore, exclusively, a pearl necklace.

Miranda★ was also British, but she remained silent most of the time. She had a beautiful red mane, longer than the hairstyle of her *Sex and the City* doppelganger. Dark freckles ran across her nose, and she sometimes wore a clean, maroon Harvard jumper that felt fitting if she was to fill the Miranda role in my fantasy. I got the sense, using my Sherlock Holmes eavesdropping skills, that she hated attending the mothers' group. I had my eye on her as a potential entry point, thinking she'd want to spice things up in a group she seemed to find quite boring.

Carrie★ was Australian, the youngest in the group, and the resident photographer. I didn't know it for sure, but I decided she was probably a mummy influencer. She was always taking pictures of the kids and would usually pull her daughter away for mummy-and-me photoshoots. The rest of the crew didn't seem to mind. She had brown hair with chunky blonde highlights, wore round glasses and seemed to have a wardrobe entirely full of jumpsuits.

Finally there was Samantha*, my ultimate girl crush. She was Australian, like Carrie. She was always the last to arrive and made a big fuss about it, blaming traffic or her husband or the baby she often held under her arm like a clutch. She seemed the least interested in parenting as a topic of conversation, with her go-to line being, 'Let's talk about something else.' But it was her fashion sense that really drew me in. She clearly worked in a creative industry, arriving in experimental looks with clashing patterns that shouldn't have worked but totally did. I had learned from eavesdropping that she'd lived in New York City. If there was any chance I could gain an invitation to the Sexless in the City group, I decided it would be through her – but that wasn't how things played out.

*

My first few attempts at a formal introduction were complete busts. I was in the habit of setting up a blanket near the water fountain just in case one of the ladies needed to fill up her bottle, so that was where my initial interactions with them occurred.

I spoke to Miranda first. She said, 'Twins?' as she passed by.

I froze and just said, 'Twins!' right back at her.

She offered up an 'adorable' and kept on walking. I don't blame her.

Cooper and me sitting on a blanket in the park near the water fountain. My expression says it all.

Then I told Samantha that the water fountain was broken. I thought this was a clever way to start a conversation in my American accent, hoping that would kickstart an hour-long discussion of our love affairs with SoHo shopping and celebrity spotting. But she just thanked me and walked away.

My first real interaction happened when I least expected it, on a Monday. The twins were getting to an age where I could plop them on top of a slide and slowly support them down to the bottom. They obviously didn't give me much in return at nine to ten months old, but I had a feeling the activity was stimulating. One day, I performed the slide routine with one child while the other sat up on the artificial turf beneath the equipment. Charlotte appeared and asked if I wanted a hand.

'That's very sweet of you, thank you,' I replied calmly, freaking out on the inside.

As she assisted in lifting Stella up and down the slide, we began to talk. It turned out she lived locally, which explained why she was at the park without the others. She had moved to Sydney from London two years prior for her husband's job. She had previously worked in publishing but stepped away to parent her first child, a daughter sleeping in a nearby pram.

We totally hit it off. She was laughing at all my jokes, I was laughing at hers, and our banter flowed naturally. We spent a decent chunk of two hours parenting each other's kids in the way good friends do without being asked to.

I felt like now was the perfect time to bring up the group. 'I've seen you around the park before – with three other women?'

'Yeah, that's my mothers' group. It used to be much larger, but it's slowly dwindled its way down to just the four of us.'

I saw my chance, and I took it. 'Any chance you're accepting applications?'

She paused and looked my way, obviously made awkward by the request. 'Well, we actually just discussed letting a dad into the group a few weeks back. But a couple of the other ladies felt a bit uncomfortable with it, even with having their husbands swap in.'

'Oh, of course. I totally get it.'

'Yeah ... it's just that, well, we talk about a lot of personal stuff. You know, ladies' things. And we agreed – even though I don't fully agree – it's best to keep the group tight.'

There it was: the formal rejection, the 'you can't sit with us' moment I had feared. I wasn't welcome in their group, not now and not ever. And for some strange reason, this felt like a formal rejection from all mothers' groups. I had this nasty narrative in the back of my head, a persistent voice that told me women wouldn't accept me as a stay-at-home parent. I'd had close friends who were men all of my life, but most of them were childless, give or take a few. Women were my safe space throughout adolescence and into adulthood, so I believed they would be the key to my happiness as I traversed the parenting journey. I didn't need the acceptance of these four local mums, but I desperately wanted it. I was still new to this city and spent ninety per cent of my time in Balmain. The thought of having to go outside of that safety net felt, at the time, unbearable. Plus, it was the role of mother that I most identified with; it was the role, on paper, that I was playing. I wanted to join a group of mothers. That specific mothers' group in that specific park in that specific neighbourhood. I felt like a very important door was being closed in my face, letting me know I would never be welcomed into this part of the parenting community.

I know I could have tried a lot harder. In retrospect, there's a long list of 'could haves'. I could have asked them to reconsider adding a gay man. I could have pulled at her heartstrings and said, 'Without a mother in our home, I need close female friends to assist as Stella and Cooper grow up.' I could have found other local groups of parents with children a bit older or younger than mine. I could have kept googling and making more phone calls and asking strangers for advice. I could have signed up for more baby classes, attended more 'Mums & Bubs' movie sessions or been more proactive at the playground. But I didn't. I felt like a kid being picked last for a schoolyard game, except I wasn't allowed to play at all. So just like when I would eat alone in the nurse's office before finding friends in primary school, I decided to stick to myself.

I ended up spending my first eight months in Australia without any real parenting friends. I made connections – like Jen and Grace – at parties and classes, but for whatever reason I wasn't able to translate those interactions into friendships. When I attended two Rainbow Families meet-ups – a community for local queer parents, who met at a playcentre – I just couldn't find my people. I started to wonder if it was my fault. Was I not cut out to be friends with other parents, especially mothers?

I've thought through the story of the Sexless and the City ladies many times, attempting to analyse the situation with empathy. I believe that mums deserve safe spaces to discuss the most intimate details of their parenting journeys and I also believe that they were wrong to exclude me because I'm a man.

It's my angry ego talking, but I just know that they would have benefited from having another perspective in the group, and I could have benefited from having theirs. I could have given them permission to talk more freely with their partners. I would have challenged and supported them, while offering a fresh point of view. Having a cheeky Stanford Blatch – Carrie's best gay friend on the show – to accompany them on their sexless adventures would have absolutely broadened their horizons.

If parents aren't talking out loud together on a regular basis about the rude realities of raising children, then how are we supposed to survive this roller-coaster ride? I'm not sure we can. Which is why I'm a firm supporter of changing all mothers' groups to parenting groups, so that lonely fathers like me never have to slip through the cracks again.

Chapter Fourteen

The Bubble

It was August 2018, a month before the twins turned one, and I was cooking dinner for the family in the kitchen. I use the term 'cooking' loosely, because I was just lazily boiling pasta and warming up a half-empty bottle of Dolmio sauce that may or may not have been sitting in the fridge for a month. Stella had recently been appointed to the role of my sous-chef. We were attached at the hip. She was at the age where her hair length still made her look fairly androgynous. When I looked at her, I saw myself as a child. It was like looking into a much more youthful mirror. She enjoyed following me around, refusing to properly crawl but instead pulling herself forward with one leg in front and the other behind her in a semi-split. I didn't mind the company, so I liked to place her in a highchair behind me so she could gnaw on a rusk and provide me with emotional support.

'It's starting to bubble, sous-chef. Should I add the pasta now?' I asked.

'Dadadadadadada!' she replied.

'It's chef. Call me chef at work, please,' I joked.

Josh was in the living room watching Cooper play in a new ball pit, a gift we had given the twins for surviving Tresillian's sleep-training boot camp. Cooper had recently discovered the power of his boisterous cackle and its ability to bring any adult to their knees. I could hear his giggles harmonising with his father's, like a duelling piano performance of father-son laughter bouncing around the room.

Before Josh had gone on-air for his radio show that morning, he'd texted me to wish me luck for the day ahead, and also asked if I could run a load of laundry. *And if you have time*, the message continued, *could you grab some groceries so we don't order takeaway all weekend long?* In true Sean Szeps fashion, I placed his message at the back of my mind in the 'deal with this later' folder; the one that would quickly be buried under the 'keep your children entertained' hard drive and subsequently forgotten about.

'Did you get a chance to wash that shirt, babe?' he now hollered from the living room, over the gurgling sounds of salted water coming to a boil.

'Oh shit. I slept during their naps and then was at the park, and I just forgot.'

'It's okay, I'll throw it in right now.'

Josh had always been extremely patient with me – some might argue a little too patient. He obviously loved a lot of things about me, but my ability to respond to texts and keep up with chores was certainly not on the list. I had never been good at advance planning or responding punctually, and since having children and moving to Australia, things had been getting worse and worse.

I poked my head out of the kitchen. 'I'm really sorry!'

'It's fine! I'm not worried about it.'

But *I* was worried about it. I just couldn't figure out a way to do anything outside of keeping the children entertained. Every other responsibility felt like an impossible task that was weighing down an already difficult day.

'You grabbed the weekend groceries, right?' he asked, raising his eyebrows with intrigue.

'I did … not get the groceries. But I can go right now.'

'It's okay, we can just do it together in the morning.' He gave a half-smile and turned back to Cooper.

Josh never showed signs of frustration. He never once raised his voice or made me feel bad about dropping the ball, but I knew I was letting him down. Worse yet, I knew I was letting myself down. I could feel the emotions climbing from the depths of my chest towards my face, equal parts embarrassment and shame. I had been working double time to suppress the belief that I was, even with the Zoloft, struggling to keep up with the day-to-day tasks of raising kids and running a house. If it wasn't the missed groceries, it was the messy house; if it wasn't the messy house, it was the missed payment for the baby sensory class. Having sought treatment, I felt like I couldn't keep blaming my sleep deprivation or the depression. Maybe I just wasn't fit for the role of stay-at-home parent.

I had decided long before the children were born that I was going to play the role of a mother. In my mind, one of us needed to be the mother – my mother – and, partly based on my history of fangirling over moms, I thought it should be me. This meant I would be doing everything my mom once had.

I made it clear to Josh, on multiple occasions, that I would be brilliant at the job – some might say I was cocky about it. I specifically recall telling Josh, shortly after we decided to pursue the surrogacy route, that I had been 'preparing for this role my entire life'. When he chuckled and asked if I wanted to discuss how we might handle challenges like sleep training and work–life balance, I brushed it all off. 'There are very few people as prepared for this as I am,' I assured him. 'We have nothing to worry about.'

I was the one, all those months ago, who had wanted to be a stay-at-home parent. I had always thought of myself as being just like Mom, a badge of honour I wore proudly. We had the same strengths and similar weaknesses, so why wouldn't we have near-identical parenting abilities? So I'd raised my hand and walked away from a successful career in advertising.

I was also the one who'd had a mental breakdown. And now I couldn't even follow through on the day-to-day responsibilities of helping to run a household. My mother had done it alone, so why wasn't I capable of doing it, even after getting help?

Josh was more than pulling his weight, and he too was experiencing transition fatigue. On top of juggling a new high-stress, high-stakes, high-visibility job, he had moved back home after twelve years away and was re-establishing old friendships. The pressure to deliver professionally was absolutely weighing on him, though he didn't share this with me. He kept quiet because he was busy focusing on my mental health. A stand-up bloke, I know.

He was an involved husband and father. He'd taken charge of the family finances, managing our difficult shift from being a two-income couple to a one-income family with twins. On top of that, he was in charge of most of the family admin: getting Australian passports for the kids, signing us up for Medicare, finding an immigration lawyer to handle my visa, and many other tasks. Because I had the twins during the day, Josh would take charge as soon as he arrived home, letting me relax in our bedroom. He also fell into a routine of taking the kids out of the house each Saturday and Sunday morning to let me sleep. I felt terrible that every time I dropped the ball, he added another side dish to his already full plate. But he wasn't blaming me: he had his own world of postnatal stress, gloom and exhaustion. As far as he was concerned, the two of us were clinging on together for dear life.

If this had been the first time I'd dropped the ball, I probably would have brushed it all off. But one mistake had become ten, and then ten had become … well, I had lost count. As the pasta water bubbled over the edge of the pot, I realised I couldn't take it any longer. I turned off the stove, hid behind Stella's highchair, tucked my head beneath her little kicking feet and began to cry.

Josh heard my hushed tears, though, and rushed into the kitchen. 'What's wrong, monkey?' he asked.

'I hate how bad I am at this job.'

'Cooking pasta?' he asked.

'No. I thought Tresillian would fix everything. I thought the medicine would be an instant solution, but I can't be a stay-at-home parent. I can't do it like my mom did.'

'Hey, hey, come here.' He lifted me up off the ground and held me close. 'We can figure this out together.'

That night, while the kids slept, we sat at our dining table and talked. Josh led the conversation, and I followed along like a helpless puppy.

'What's currently on your plate?' he asked.

'Cooking, shopping, laundry, cleaning and everything kids-related.'

'And which of those things don't you want to do anymore?'

'I mean … I can do all of them.'

'I know you *can* do all of them, monkey. But maybe not all at once? It's a big list. And even if you *could* do it, I want to know which ones you *don't* want to do. Or maybe a better question is, what's the one thing I can take off your plate to alleviate some pressure?'

'I hate doing the laundry – I'm terrible at folding it, and this whole not-having-a-dryer thing is really hard for me. What rental doesn't come with a dryer? Hanging them on an outdoor washing line like it's the pre-industrial era is ruining my days.'

'Okay, this is a great start. I'll take over the laundry. Anything else?'

We worked through a list of my responsibilities. He took over half of the cooking days and decided to take ownership of the weekly grocery shop. Then the tables turned: he said he wasn't enjoying doing the dishes and felt like he was filling every free second with the kids, so we agreed to give him one evening off a week and one weekend morning to sleep in.

'Now, when you say you're bad at this job,' he said, 'what exactly do you mean?'

'I thought all of this parenting stuff would come more naturally to me. My mom was so good at it, and I have so much experience with kids, so it's shocked me how poorly I've been handling it all. I thought that when the meds kicked in, I'd get a second wind. But it's just not happening. I'm not as good at this as Mom is. I love our kids, obviously, but I love myself, too. I just can't keep going on like this, not for the long haul.'

'Now we're getting somewhere.' Josh stood up and gave me a massive bearhug. 'When you're open and honest like this, you're at your very best. Now that this is out in the open, we can do something about it.'

★

That was the first of many conversations, each led by Josh, where we sat down to negotiate our responsibilities and needs. We decided to rewrite the parenting script together, pretending like it had never existed. What had started off as a simple conversation about chores evolved into a total rehaul of our relationship. It was fucking fabulous.

Over the course of several weeks, we fleshed out a plan. First, we talked about the things we both enjoyed most in our lives. We asked ourselves what things – outside of each other and the kids – felt like non-negotiables if we were going to feel fulfilled. Then we agreed on one activity for each of us to hold sacred, personal training for Josh and Pilates for me, and scheduled them into our calendar. We were prioritising each other's happiness.

Second, we looked at our day-to-day family responsibilities. After we had each taken a couple of things off the other's plate, we worked through the rest of the list, making sure it was balanced: equal parts things we were okay with and things we disliked.

Third, we introduced a date night once a week. That meant finding a babysitter, but we agreed it was the right thing to do to make sure our relationship remained strong.

Fourth, we talked about our sex life, our diet and how often we were watching television versus reading or talking – and then we agreed it was time to rethink our relationship to technology. We began sleeping with our mobile phones outside of our bedroom so we had the best chance possible to be well rested.

Finally, we agreed I should go back to work.

The initial insight had come during a therapy session in which I said, 'But my mother didn't work,' when defending my desire to power through the discomfort of being a stay-at-home father.

When my therapist replied, 'But you're not your mother,' it stopped me in my tracks. She had said this before, in various ways, but this time it hit differently. Maybe it was her tone, maybe it was the post-Zoloft clarity, or maybe I was just finally willing to listen.

I started to come to terms with the fact I wasn't the same as her, and that this was okay. Forcing myself to stay at home and muddle through unhappiness wasn't making me a good dad. I needed to lean into my own strengths, just as she had – only then could I hope to become as wonderful a parent and partner as she was. I threw the desire to copy my mother out the window and focused on creating a role that catered to me in all my uniqueness.

I was clearly struggling to find friends at the playground, and I thought diving back into an office environment might be a gateway to relationships with like-minded creatives. I had set out to stay at home with the twins for two years, but eleven months would have to do. Did I still feel like a failure at some level? Yeah, of course I did. But I knew that if finding friends and achieving career goals could unlock some happiness, then I would become a better dad.

The only problem I could foresee, other than the annoying application and interview process, was that I wanted to work part-time. I wasn't nailing stay-at-home parenting, but I loved my children and was enjoying watching them grow. I also knew that I'd look back on this time with them and regret not being around more, so I wanted to remain at home a few days a week. But advertising agencies weren't great at offering part-time positions. When I hunted for part-time director-level roles, I came up empty-handed. I guess I should have predicted that I'd need to take a position cut, so I changed my expectations.

One night, Josh shared a list of Aussie connections with me. He suggested that I grab a coffee with a few of his mates to pick their brains about how my skills might best be of use in Australia. I sent out five emails.

The first response I got was from Eric Stephens. He and Josh had been friends for nearly two decades, meeting when Josh was a voiceover artist and Eric hired him to do some advertising work. Eric, an American who had put down roots in Oz, was the founder and owner of a creative agency, True Sydney. It was a small shop, maybe ten people at the time.

When I went in to have a coffee with Eric, I wasn't in a job interview state of mind. I had left the States on a high, having worked with some of the largest brands in the world, so I wanted to continue that trajectory at a large international agency.

Eric was one of the most illuminating people that I'd ever met. He had star power, balancing a casual calmness that put me at ease with a wealth of knowledge that kept me on my toes. Within minutes of arriving at his office, I found myself wanting to impress him. I didn't know a lot about True, but I wanted to work with him in some capacity based solely on his impressive energy.

He was a father of five girls, and his wife worked part-time in the business, heading up the finance team. It was instantly clear that he, more than most male professionals I had worked with, understood the sacrifices parents make in order to chase their professional dreams.

'Sean, what is it going to take to get you to come and work here?' Eric asked boldly.

I brought my NYC grit to the exchange. 'I have a feeling you can't afford me.'

'Try me,' he replied without skipping a beat, unwilling to back down.

We played a cat-and-mouse game for the rest of the meeting. I was intrigued and inspired, but I also didn't want to just take the first job that came my way, so I decided to be honest. I told him I was only looking for part-time work and would be interviewing at a lot of other agencies. I had plans to shake his hand, walk out of the room and leverage the meeting as a jumping-off point. This was a practice date, basically, an opportunity to flex my interview muscles and regain some of the fierce confidence I'd displayed in the States.

But then Eric ended the meeting with a short monologue, perhaps a last-ditch effort to win me over. 'Working in this industry as a parent, especially one who wants to be involved at home, is hard. I've seen it, and you've seen it too. The big agencies expect more than a parent should be willing to offer. It's the sad truth. When I started True, I had parents in mind because I had newborn triplets at home. I've always thought since those early days of growing this company from my bedroom that no one works harder than a stay-at-home parent. If that's what you're looking to do, this can be the place for you to do it. One day a week, two or even more – you name it. We can pick hours that suit the twins' schedule. Come in early, beat the young crowd, work your ass off and then leave before everyone else. From one parent to another, I get that this will be hard. But it doesn't have to be impossible, Sean. You should be able to raise your kids and do work that you love.'

I didn't need to hear another word, instantly knowing I would accept any position working for Eric at True. I wasn't naive to the struggles that lay ahead, but his offer made it all a lot less daunting, and it seemed like an opportunity I might never get again.

Later that day, I emailed Eric. *I think tiptoeing back into the workforce with True is an ideal situation – for both of us*, I said, among other things.

He replied the next day with, *Dude, this is the best bit of news I've seen today, or yesterday or the day before.*

It was official: I was re-entering the workforce.

Around that time, Josh invited one of his closest friends, Rachel Corbett, over to our place for a glass of wine. She was head of the Mamamia Podcast Network. When I'd said I wanted to go back to work, I hadn't been thinking of entering a new industry; I certainly hadn't thought of taking on two part-time jobs. But when Rachel asked if I would consider coming in to audition for the parenting podcast she was creating, I remembered my father-in-law's wise words. Performing was in my bones – maybe I could perform as a podcaster, too.

The following week, I arrived early for the audition and was greeted by Rachel, who ushered me into an empty studio. It was a tiny room, the size of a walk-in closet, with sound-proof padding on the walls and door, and a small circular table that sat in the centre of the space. It was dark, hot and very quiet.

A few minutes later, a beautiful brunette walked in. She looked like a model: her hair was freshly blown and coiffed to one side, her makeup flawlessly set, and her outfit immaculate from head to toe. She posed against the doorframe and then dropped her designer purse on the desk between us, holding her arms out to me. 'Hi, I'm Zoe Marshall. I'm a hugger. I hope that's okay!'

'I'm a hugger, too. I'm Sean Szeps. It's nice to meet you!'

We settled in and put our headphones on while we awaited directions from Rachel. I'll never forget Zoe leaning across the table and whispering to me, 'Let's just pretend we're grabbing coffee and no one else is listening.'

Zoe and I were, on paper, polar opposites. She was a straight woman married to a famous footballer and seemed well-off. I was gay, married to a radio presenter and could barely afford a large cup of coffee. She was visual perfection, and I rolled into the studio wearing a two-year-old H&M jumpsuit. But Zoe and I had an instant connection that surprised us both. In that tiny studio, our conversation flowed naturally and a bond was formed. With equal parts comedic banter and brutal honesty about her parenting experiences, Zoe wasn't afraid to address her honest concerns with motherhood. Her words were the perfect antidote to the struggles I'd experienced the year prior.

The rest, as they say, is history. Rachel saw something special in us that day and decided to give us the job, so we started recording *The Baby Bubble* later that month. On the day of its release, the podcast shot to number one on the charts. Shortly after, Josh and I were invited onto Mia Freedman's podcast, *No Filter*, to share the story of our path to parenthood. Then ABC TV's *The Drum* asked me to be a panellist on an episode called 'Parenting in the 21st Century'. These opportunities introduced me to a whole new group of Australian parents. Overnight, my Instagram audience grew from 2k to 5k, and soon it was 10k.

Meanwhile, I was becoming increasingly capable of dealing with the pressures of parenthood. The children started sleeping better, which meant I was sleeping better. I was making friends at True and developing a serious bond with Zoe, unlike any I had formed since leaving the States. I rediscovered my pre-parenting creative spirit and began doing daily craft projects with the twins: homemade playdough, finger painting and water colouring. My relationship with my mother was stronger than ever and my husband and I were closer than we had been in years. With the first year of parenthood officially behind me, it seemed that the tide was finally turning. The best, I prayed, was yet to come.

Zoe Marshall. My work wife, my bosom buddy, the Aussie Bonnie to my American Clyde.

Chapter Fifteen

The Godfather

When my brother asked me to be the godfather of his first-born child, I cried hysterically for much longer than is universally considered appropriate. The embarrassing marathon of tears didn't happen immediately – I worked my way up to it. First I gasped, then I collapsed onto the table directly in front of my iPhone, which I had propped up against a fancy Glasshouse candle I was reluctant to use. I then slammed my forehead a few times on the table, shouting, 'Oh my god! Oh my god!' For some, this performance might have seemed dramatic. But to my brother, Steven, and sister-in-law, Kayla, this was just another Tuesday.

It was when Cooper interrupted my performance with a playful squeal that I really began to cry. I often thought of my brother when I saw Cooper – I was raising his mini-me.

Steven asking me to be the godfather of his daughter was one of the biggest surprises of my adult life. Not like when he'd asked me to be his best man, which I had been anticipating from the ripe old age of ten. Not like when he'd announced that he and Kayla were getting married, which everyone had been expecting. And not like when he told me his wife was pregnant, which he had hinted at earlier. I cried at all of those announcements, but more out of duty and a general inability to manage positive emotions than genuine shock. But I hadn't seen this in my cards.

I had thought – that is to say, I'd been entirely certain – that I had forfeited any chance at being appointed to the Catholic role of godfather when I came out as gay. Surely I had confirmed somewhere along the line that my flamboyant exit from the Church and loud promises to 'never step foot in that fucking place again' barred me from re-entry, yet here we were.

My first niece, Leah, who had been earth-side for only a few short months, was going to be baptised and welcomed into the Christian church. And I was going to be there with her parents, standing beside them as her godfather. That, especially for a Catholic, really meant something. It was a special position reserved only for the closest of friends or family members. Someone who understood the faith and cared for the family. Someone who could usher the child into the faith and act as a supporting moral compass as they grew.

'So is that a yes?' Kayla asked with a giggle.

'Of course that's a yes!' I replied, lifting my head off the table and wiping snot across the front of my t-shirt.

'Good, because you don't have a choice,' my brother joked.

★

My 'big brother' Steven is both younger and taller than me. Our 15.6-centimetre height difference has made lots of people – strangers and acquaintances alike – confident of an incorrect age order. But that isn't the only reason why I refer to him as my big brother.

Steven displays much more maturity than I do. In stark contrast to me, with my dirty sense of humour and reputation as a party animal, my brother arrived on planet earth with a much more serious approach to life. I insert my opinion into every conversation; he's fine sitting back and listening. I jump around from job to job; he's remained at the same company since graduating from college. He's focused, grounded and spends more time thinking of others than himself. My favourite subject is me.

For a very tall and masculine man, my brother has always been unusually empathetic. When I had regular anxiety attacks growing up, he instinctively knew to hug me tight without pause, to help slow down my heart rate. If I watched a scary movie and couldn't sleep, he'd welcome me into his room; I'd open the door and, without any dialogue required, he'd lift up his sheets and roll over to make room for me. When I was broken up with unexpectedly in college, he cradled me like a small child until I passed out in his arms; he even slept on the floor of my room for two days until he was confident I could be left alone again. He's always stayed up and waited for me to come home when I'm out partying. He did this for such a long time growing up, with a puke bucket in hand and a cup of ice-water by the side of my bed, that his sleep cycle was permanently altered.

Steven (left) and I were always stuck together. Not by force, but by choice.

There's one other reason why I see Steven as my big brother: he was forced into that role the second I came out as gay.

In high school I had built up a really solid reputation. The bullies who had ruined my life in middle school were, serendipitously, destroyed by puberty; the King of Bullies had lost his prepubescent good looks, and with them his powerful position. Meanwhile, the groundwork I had laid in the closet was finally paying off. I had been on the football team and was protected by the captains, who thought of me as their little brother. I was beloved by most straight boys for my sense of humour and connection to the girls they wanted to hook up with, and I was the top breaststroker on the swim team. My very best friends, a trio of talented girls named Sarah, Brittany and Rebecca, had a reputation for making people laugh. We hovered directly below the popular clique and above the misfits, a safe space to occupy in the American high school hierarchy. My flamboyance, which also occupied a safe middle ground, made me less of an obvious target than, say, the boy from a few grades above me who came out after graduating and instantly started wearing fishnets and face glitter.

When I finally announced to the world that I was bi and then later gay, it seemed like a non-issue at my school.

'I heard you were gay?' a basketballer said to me in the hallway a few days after the news went public.

'Yeah, that's true,' I replied.

'Cool. I thought it was true, but I wanted to ask. Do you have a boyfriend or something?'

'No.'

'You're brave, Gallerani. Good for you.'

Throughout the rest of my time at school, I certainly was thought of as 'the gay kid'. But because I owned it with confidence and was surrounded by people who supported me, bullies weren't able to use it against me like they had in middle school. If they shouted, 'What, are you gay or something?' at me in the hallway, I'd shout back, 'Yeah I fucking am – any other stupid questions?' The crowds would cheer, and the bully would disappear.

In my senior year, I was crowned prom king. That scared little fruit cup who had cowered in the church pews, petrified to walk in the front door of his middle school – the one who'd hidden with shame in the closet for years, praying his truth would never be leaked around town – was not just out of the closet but was also being celebrated by his peers. That, my friends, is a fairytale ending to a challenging adolescence.

But while the bullies were avoiding me, they were making a direct course for my brother. They couldn't use my gayness against me anymore because I was out of the closet and semi-popular, so instead of just dropping the subject and moving on, they shifted their focus to Steven.

While I was in the process of coming out, Steven was forced to become my PR manager at school. If students were uncomfortable talking to me about my potential gayness, they'd simply walk right up to him in the middle of class and demand he answer their queries. As if it wasn't hard enough to be a thirteen-year-old boy at high school, living in the educational shadows of his very smart and charismatic older brother, Steven took on the weight of public confusion about my sexuality and the homophobia that came with it.

'Yo, Steven, is your brother gay?' they'd ask.

'Yeah, why?' he would reply.

'Fucking gross.'

We've always been extremely close, Steven and I. Having to hear his classmates say nasty things about me, especially to his face, wasn't easy for him. We were raised to 'use words, not fists', so he did his best to ignore the slurs. But there's only so much a teenage boy can handle. During his four years at high school, Steven found himself in many verbal altercations concerning things people said about me. Even when I graduated and moved out of town to attend college, the frequent references to his gay brother didn't stop.

'If Sean's gay, you're probably gay too.'

'Does being gay run in the family, Gallerani?'

'Even Sean has slept with more girls than you have, and he's gay. What's your excuse?'

I won't sit here and say that what Steven had to go through was more difficult than what I dealt with. Being gay as a Roman Catholic child was an issue I struggled with for decades. In many ways, I'm still struggling with it. But in a sense, I wasn't the only one who had to come out of the closet at school.

★

In May 2019, I flew solo from Sydney to New Hampshire for Leah's Baptism. Stella and Cooper were only eighteen months old, and taking the entire family to America for a third time that year seemed like financial overkill. I had been struggling with my new work–life balance and desperately missing my family of origin, so Josh suggested I go alone and said he'd be fine parenting solo for a week. A beautiful and unexpected offer that brought me to tears.

On 1 June, I squeezed into a maroon suit and rocked up to the church. It was a tiny brick building with a large wooden cross on top, that sat on the side of a busy highway, surrounded by gorgeous green foliage. I had only been inside a few churches since leaving the faith, for weddings of dear friends or family members. When Steven and Kayla had married a few years earlier, the wedding party had arrived at the church for a rehearsal the day prior. The priest was a cheeky man in his sixties or seventies, cracking jokes and doing his best – successfully, I might add – to connect with the young wedding party. He then made a joke about 'holy water burning the sinners', which was a not-so-friendly reminder that I wasn't on Oxford Street in Sydney anymore.

From the moment my brother and sister-and-law asked me to fly home for the Baptism, to the second I stepped foot in that church, it never once crossed my mind that I wouldn't enjoy the experience. I was lost in the excitement of it all: getting a break from the kids, flying home to be a godfather, and did I mention getting a break from the kids? What wasn't to love? Plus, I had successfully suppressed enough of my religious trauma that I hadn't even considered the potential of being triggered. Sure, I had walked away from the Catholic Church. And yeah, I had a deep aversion to any song with the word 'God' in it. But I had gone to therapy and talked about my trauma a few times, so surely I was healed.

When I went into the church with my family and began walking down the aisle to find our pew, everything started to unravel. Maybe it was the organ music, or the familiar smells that hit me as I neared my seat. Maybe it was seeing my family, all five of us, back together in a church. It could have been the stained-glass windows colouring the sunlight that poured onto my seat. Maybe it was the priest smiling at me, or the frayed edges of the Bibles along the pews, just like the ones I had picked at as a kid.

The second the priest began to speak, I couldn't get one nagging thought out of my head: *What if Leah is a lesbian?*

I couldn't focus, not for a single minute of the ceremony. Most of the sermon was filled with the priest talking to the congregation about the Lord Jesus Christ looking lovingly and mercifully over Leah. He granted her new life through Baptism and welcomed her into the Church as a faithful Christian witness. But even though he was talking about my niece, I could only hear my own name.

'What name do you give your child?'

'Sean Joseph Gallerani.'

'What do you ask of God's Church for Sean Joseph?'

'Baptism.'

In my mind, the soundtrack of my adolescence started drowning out the priest's words. I was reminded of what I'd thought of back then as my nightly prayer ritual, a secret I'd kept from the world. Each and every night, after the house fell silent, I would close my eyes and picture some of the most beautiful women in the world. I'd desperately flick through a database of them to find the one who could get me hard: tall women, short women, black women or white women. Would red hair excite me, or maybe a shaved head? But night after night, I fell short –

well, my penis did. Then, no matter how hard I tried to stop them, my impulses would drag me towards men. I'd change the channel in my mind hundreds of times a night, forcefully imagining toilet bowls and dead deer. But, like it had in every gay boy before me, the channel always flicked back to what my body truly desired. I'd reluctantly give in. And, like Jesus after His crucifixion, it would rise.

When it fell, I would pray, 'Forgive me, Father, for I have sinned. I am gay. The devil is inside me, forcing me to think the very worst thoughts – thoughts I cannot control. I'm worried, God, that I will act on them again. I'm sorry for my sins. I am sinning against you, and I should love you above all other things. I need your help, Father. Please, Father. Make me straight, Father. I will do anything for you. I will dedicate my entire life to your service. I will become a priest and spread your gospel around the world. I will marry a woman and have children and raise them to be good Catholics. I will never look like that at a man again. Please, God. Fix me, God. Remove the devil from inside this disgusting body.'

But He never did. Life as I knew it was over. After my time on earth I was destined for eternal torture, so what was the point of living?

That was when *it* began. After years of these nightly prayers, my bed became a fearful place. The stress would build up inside me without a place to go. Over time, I found that I needed another physical outlet if I was ever going to sleep. I began cutting: shallow cuts at first, with the head of a drawing pin, and later more deeply, with kitchen knives. Always below my belt, on my hips and thighs – that way no one would see them.

I convinced myself that the cuts would remove the gay, signalling to God that I was willing to make sacrifices for Him. But soon I became addicted to the release. The negative voice inside my head was so persistent that I found it impossible to sleep without cutting. It was the only way to turn everything off and shock my body back to reality. The welcomed pain would cause me to pass out. Finally, sleep.

At Leah's Baptism, a tear streamed down my face as I thought about the pain the Church has caused me. I quickly wiped away the tear and forced a smile. I wanted to be present – for my family, for my brother and for Leah – but I couldn't stop thinking about the nightly ritual of praying the gay away, the anxious trips to Confession, the nightmares of Hell, and the Bible under my pillow. Just as I had replaced Leah's name with my own, I began to replace myself with her in these terrible memories. I saw Leah huddled in the corner of her bedroom, running her fingers over the words 'You shall not lie with a man as with a woman. That is detestable,' in the Bible. I saw her making herself memorise these words, crying in silence, keeping secrets from her parents, and considering harming herself. I saw her walk into the church each Sunday, fearful of its power.

I didn't know who Leah would become. I didn't know how important God would be in her life as she got older. And I was projecting my childhood trauma onto her, a helpless little girl. But even though I didn't know who she would grow up to be, I was being asked to set a good example of Jesus' love for her – and I was afraid I might not be able to do that.

My family, my beautiful family, know I feel this way, I told myself. *Clearly they have simply forgotten.*

They knew, deep down, just how hard it was for me to be there. Or maybe they didn't? Maybe my lies and fake smiles had worked. Had I told my family exactly how I felt, or had I just thought the thoughts and kept the words to myself all these years? I couldn't remember. We didn't talk about the Church; maybe because it was too difficult, maybe because I was too difficult. I was sure, though, that they knew I struggled with memories of the priests who had convinced me at a young age that I was Hell-bound. My family knew I didn't believe in God anymore, and they knew exactly why.

Even with all that knowledge, they weren't at all concerned, not one of them, that the same thing could happen to Leah. The thought that they would place her in harm's way devastated me.

My anxious brain wouldn't quit. *Why am I even here?* I kept thinking. *This event is important to your brother, to your family. Leah needs someone who believes in all this bullshit. And you, most definitely, do not. Get up, walk out, text your brother to say he's made a mistake, and run.*

I picked up my phone, typed in the four-digit password and opened the messaging app. There I sat in a pew on the day of my goddaughter's Baptism, anxiously editing a godfather break-up text.

★

I never sent that text to my brother. How could I? Steven had shown me nothing but unconditional love and support through the wildest and weirdest of times. Not only had he protected me throughout our childhood and adolescence, but he'd selected me, his out-and-proud gay brother, as his best man and then as his daughter's godfather.

He'd known all along that I wasn't the typical man for the job, but he didn't care. He'd chosen me in spite of what the Church saw as my flaws, maybe even because of them. That empathy he always showed was the answer I had been looking for – I just needed to have a little myself.

I didn't believe in God anymore, but my brother and sister-in-law did. So did our parents, and so did most of our friends and family. And they loved me, just as I was. They didn't see an issue with me being a godfather, gay or not. So why did I? If Leah turned out to be a lesbian or bisexual or gender diverse, and she was feeling like a sinner, then what voice would I want her to hear? The answer was clear: mine.

Chapter Sixteen

The Drug Dealer

When the twins were two years old, we drugged them on a plane. It's not something I'm proud to admit now, but we were desperate back then.

Josh and I had been flying with Stella and Cooper a dozen times a year, mostly to see my family in the States. The more often we flew, the easier it became. We travelled light and gate-checked our double pram. Josh was an expert at finding the most child-friendly airlines, and I had become a leading authority on 'distraction bags': backpacks filled to the brim with activities to keep the kids occupied in the air. The perfect recipe proved to be an iPad, three colouring books, stickers, a notepad, stamps, Play-Doh, a tiny box of Lego, one plush toy, two picture books, a magnet game and a selection of unhealthy snacks. The horror stories of travelling with children, the ones passed down through generations of anxious flyers, were proving to be untrue … mostly.

After nearly thirty flights in those first two years, there was one thing my husband and I couldn't seem to master: the children's jet lag. It was our biggest sticking point, besides arguing about which parent needed to do what on any given flight. We adults would adjust our circadian rhythms by drinking wine, waiting for the cabin lights to dim, and then using the opportunity to get some much-needed beauty sleep. But the children, our adorable frequent flyers, were much less flexible. Upon arrival in Sydney at the end of each trip, they would be up all night and sleeping in random pockets throughout the day. I'd tried absolutely everything, but getting both kids onto the same sleep schedule was like trying to convince myself to enjoy sleeping with women.

I was juggling the normal responsibilities of keeping them alive while working tirelessly for days – sometimes weeks – to shift their schedules back to 'normal'. I began to resent Josh for not being able to help more because of his work schedule. He had a 'good life', in my eyes, running off to his job each day to communicate with adults in complete sentences, while I dealt with the impossible task of forcing tiny humans to do the opposite of what their bodies wanted them to do – well, I did this part-time along with a part-time advertising job and a podcast-hosting gig. After a few too many bitch fests where I threatened never to fly again, Josh began to search for solutions.

First he consulted our GP, who swiftly rejected any suggestion that didn't involve natural sun exposure. Josh then dove into an internet rabbit hole in search of solutions. He didn't find any easy answers. You could take an afternoon flight, eat meals on local time and force the kids outside to soak up the sun. But we had already been doing those things with very little success.

The Drug Dealer

Somewhere along the way, the topic of drugs came up. Not the fun kind – though that would have been welcomed by the adults at this stage – but medications that cause drowsiness, like Phenergan and Benadryl. Oh my!

This is a highly sensitive subject, both off and online, but so is everything else. You can't have a conversation about baby-led weaning without offending half the Western world, so we didn't base parenting decisions on the reactions of keyboard warriors. We were finally convinced by a friend's mother – an adoring grandmother, no less – that a small dose of Phenergan would help to ease stress and encourage sleep in little kids, supporting them to get back to the desired routine. 'That's what we did when our kids were younger,' she said to Josh on a weekend family holiday. Because I was always taught to respect my elders, especially experienced grandmothers, I decided it would be rude to disagree.

This grandmother was convinced, my husband was convinced, and a few random bloggers three pages deep into a Google search were convinced. So the decision was made: we'd be drugging our toddlers on our next long-haul flight.

I mean, parents used to give their kids bourbon to put them to sleep, I thought to myself. *And they turned out totally fine … I think. What's the worst that could happen?* If I could go back and punch myself in the face, I absolutely would.

There are five things I'd like you to take into consideration before labelling me as a drug-pushing parent and burning this book.

One: We were first-time fathers of twin toddlers. At this stage of our parenting journey, we were making hundreds of micro-decisions a day, each of them as seemingly important as the last. We had a problem, one of many, and people we trusted had a solution that they had successfully trialled. We took the advice and we flew with it. Pun intended.

Two: I really wasn't in the best mindset those first couple of years of parenting. Josh was in survival mode, desperate to make me happy. He was juggling three full-time jobs: his prestigious radio gig at the ABC, being a first-time father to twin toddlers, and keeping me, his not-so-prestigious husband, in a sane-enough state of mind. We were much more eager than the average human to find a quick fix. I was one toddler tantrum away from sending the kids to boarding school, so we were in fight-or-flight mode. Again, pun intended.

Three: We were stubbornly committed to making this whole travelling-with-kids thing work. Josh had promised himself that he would enable my parents to see their grandkids as frequently as they would have if we'd stayed in California. And he was a world-class 'travel hacker': someone willing to dedicate the time to working within the rules set up by airlines and credit card companies in order to 'hack' into free or highly discounted flights and upgrades. The twins and I were benefiting greatly from the fruits of Josh's labour.

Four: We were flying 10,090 miles from Sydney to Boston twice a year. There was no easy way for me to visit my family of origin: no direct flight, no child-friendly routes, no magical travel hack that would carve off flying hours. We needed a solution that would keep both our children periodically asleep during those twenty-four to fifty hour hauls.

Five. As someone with often debilitating social anxiety, I preferred to avoid large groups of people (aka airports) and large groups of people in confined spaces (aka aircraft).

All of this is to say that I was in over my head. Not just with parenting – because, duh, who isn't in over their head with parenting – but with flying in general. Which is why I took a back seat on deciding whether or not my children should be taking drugs at the ripe old age of two.

★

The airline was Jetstar and the flight in question was JQ62, an eight and a half hour trip from Ho Chi Minh City to Sydney. We were flying home after a few weeks with my family and had just spent the day napping at a hotel, taking a riverboat trip, introducing the children to another culture, and inching our way towards the Sydney time zone.

It had been a disaster. Our hotel nap ran over after we hit snooze on our alarms. The children wailed all boat-ride long, throwing sweaty tantrum after sweaty tantrum. Clearly the red-eye flight was going to be a struggle. That was when we *both* agreed – an important detail – that we'd give each twin some Phenergan to help them rest.

We boarded the plane early, set ourselves up in our seats near the back, and gave a very small dose to each of the twins after take-off. Phenergan went into a syringe and down the gullets of our tiny humans, just as the cabin lights were dimmed. We looked into each other's eyes, Josh and I, like soldiers about to ship off to war.

We weren't naive dummies – well, Josh definitely wasn't. He knew that in rare cases, the drug caused not drowsiness but hyperactivity. And I knew … well, I knew absolutely nothing. It wasn't that Josh hadn't communicated the potential side effects to me; in fact, I'd asked him what they were, multiple times. But I was hoping for a 'there's a one hundred per cent success rate' and 'nothing bad has ever happened to anyone in the history of its usage', so when 'in rare cases' fell from his mouth, I stopped listening. I know, I know – it's something I'm still working on with my therapist.

Josh and Cooper were seated together across the aisle from me and Stella. When Cooper fell asleep fairly quickly, Josh took this as his cue to fall asleep too. But Stella remained wide awake. She watched the iPad, requesting to change the show every fifteen minutes. Then she got bored of the screen. I noticed she was a bit fidgety, tugging at her clothes and touching her hair, but I ignored the signs and stepped into the role of Super Parent to tire her out. I pulled out colouring books and pencils, Play-Doh and Lego. But nothing could hold her attention for longer than a few minutes. In the dark, quiet cabin, we walked around and then had a seated dance party. I even let her crawl on the floor. But nothing – I repeat nothing – was tiring her out.

The less tired she was, the more irritated I became. Not at her, of course – she was just a helpless little nugget navigating the world at the hands of her drug-pushing fathers. But Josh was fair game. He was the Frequent Flyer, he was the Master Mind, he was the Drug-Dealing Dad. And there I was, a sweet naive drug mule who was somehow stuck with a one in a million – I made up that statistic – side effect.

The Drug Dealer

So I did what any rational human would do amid this stress and discomfort: I whacked my sleeping husband in the face and forced him to switch children with me. I grabbed sleeping Cooper off his half-asleep father and cuddled him close, instantly falling asleep. Finally, after twenty-four hours with only interrupted pockets of rest, I was going to get some well-deserved shut-eye. *Josh*, I thought as I drifted off, *will benefit from all the hard work I've just put in. The second he grabs her, she'll fall fast asleep. All will be good in the world. Happily ever af–*

As soon as my eyes closed – god knows how many hours later it actually was – I was awakened by the wailing of a child nearby. *Can't that parent get their shit together*, I thought, *and quiet their annoying little monst–*

It hit me: that annoying little monster was *my* annoying little monster, and I was the annoying not-so-little parent who desperately needed to get their shit together.

Someone tapped me on the shoulder. It was Josh. 'I've tried absolutely everything, and I've tried to let you sleep as long as I can, but I'm at my wit's end. She's psychotic. I can't keep her under my control for the entire rest of the flight. Can we share?'

He pushed Stella back into my arms, and the discomfort of being woken for the second time in twenty-four hours made me see red. 'You shouldn't have given her the fucking medicine.'

'Don't blame this on me,' he shot across the aisle in an aggressive whisper.

'I *am* going to blame this on you. I never would have given her that shit on my own.'

'And yet, *we* did, Sean. *We* did give it to her. Take a deep breath, focus on her.'

I nodded, then used every trick in my parenting toolbelt to keep her calm, channelling my mother.

'I spy with my little eye ...'

cries

'I'm thinking of an animal with a long neck ...'

cries again

'Five little ducks went out one day.'

cries louder than ever before

It became evident that what she really needed was never to have taken the drug in the first place. The reality set in of what she must be experiencing. I had done many drugs of many different kinds, so I knew exactly how scary it was to feel like you were out of control with no solution in sight. We had made a massive mistake.

I was force-feeding her water and encouraging her to eat all the carbs I could get my hands on, thinking they would soak up the medicine and she'd calm down. But she was only getting more upset. Then she started to scream at the top of her lungs. Her bellow pierced the air, like she had been stung by a bee. Everyone around us was sleeping – or trying to, at least – so the stress building up inside me popped out the top of my head.

I rushed Stella down the aisle in search of something, anything. Just then, the bathroom sign switched from red to green, and a young woman stepped out and held the door for me. I dove inside to hide. I wasn't thinking straight, obviously, and convinced myself that people wouldn't be able to hear Stella from inside the loo.

I can stay in here for the rest of the flight if I have to, I thought. *She can cry as loud as she wants. Who's going to try and stop us?*

I watched my daughter transform from tiny human to rabid animal. Her eyes bulged, and she was twisting her head from side to side like she was desperately searching for something. My elaborate 'shhhing' and 'please be quiet' dance did absolutely nothing. I dressed myself up in toilet paper to make her laugh; I splashed us with tap water and made funny faces in the mirror to keep her distracted. But I really had to poop – terrible timing, I know. I convinced myself that the best strategy was for me to poop while she stood on my lap, holding on to one of my hands and my head.

It was right then that Stella decided – maybe justifiably – to remove herself from the situation. She jumped up off my legs and flew directly at the bathroom wall. I tried to grab her. But all I could do was watch as the side of my daughter's face slammed into the wall. She collapsed onto the ground in front of me.

'What the literal fuck!' I cried.

The Cirque du Soleil leap of faith and sequential fall stopped her crying. Dazed, I burst into tears. I picked her up and wrapped her in my arms. 'I'm so sorry,' I whispered. 'I'm the worst father in the history of the wo–'

Just then, a flight attendant began banging on the door. 'Is everything okay? Is everything okay? Ma'am? Sir? Is everything okay in there?'

My pants were around my ankles, pee dripping down my leg as I caressed my sweet baby's head. *I* had done this to her – *me*. And Josh, of course ... mostly Josh. Now it was my job to fix it. I felt the pressure of that on my shoulders, right there in the bathroom of JQ62.

I exited the bathroom, apologised to the flight attendant and explained the situation, then walked slowly back to our seats. Josh and Cooper were fast asleep, so I set Stella up with a blanket and an iPad.

Something had to change, and it wasn't just my underwear. I was mad at myself for going along with a plan I hadn't felt wholly confident about – but even angrier that I'd allowed the situation to get the best of me. I watched as Stella finally fell asleep. Then I sat staring out the window, tears streaming from my eyes again, and made a promise to myself: I'd never give my children fucking sleep medication again.

*

That incident was an opportunity for me and Josh to talk about what wasn't working, both in our approach to travelling and in our relationship. We agreed that we didn't travel very well together, often arriving at our destinations tired and on edge with one another. But once we had settled in, we became the best versions of ourselves. Although I didn't enjoy the plane part of travelling, I loved seeing the world with our little family.

Having those honest conversations allowed me to open up about the stress that travel was causing me. I told Josh that whenever I was anxious, I found myself placing an unusual amount of unnecessary pressure on him. This made total sense to him. 'You're uncomfortable with being at the airport and on a plane,' he said, 'and the pressure of parenting is heightened when you're out of your comfort zone.'

He was right: the frustration I directed at him under those circumstances didn't exist on the ground or when I was parenting by myself. If the kids were fighting and I was alone, on or off a plane, I'd simply break up the fight and begin distracting them; there was no other choice, no other person to take on the responsibility, so the decision-making process was clear. But when we were on a plane, and Josh was sitting there while I broke up a fight, I'd find myself tossing a 'Why aren't you helping?' his way and getting annoyed at his lack of involvement. Meanwhile, he'd be frustrated at me for being a control freak and letting my anxiety ruin everyone's fun. Neither of us enjoyed flying with the other.

Over the next few months, we rethought our approach to travel. Josh suggested we explore travelling separately, an approach we now affectionately refer to as 'The Mile Apart Club' or 'Divide and Conquer'. It's not often that you pack for a family holiday, travel to the airport together, check in, hang out in the lounge, scan your boarding passes at the gate, walk across the jet bridge, board the plane and then walk in the opposite direction of your children – that is, unless you're me and my husband. One of us flies in business or first class, while the other is up the back with the kids. The one up the front arrives refreshed and immediately takes over parenting duties for the first few days after we land. And because we always switch roles on the return flight, the one who travels with the children on the outbound journey has it in the back of his head that he'll get respite on the trip home.

For us, it works perfectly. I get to remove the variable that stresses me out (him) so I can focus on what's most important to me (my sanity), while Josh gets to remove the variable that annoys him (me) so he can focus on what matters to him (the joy of travel). Afterwards we're really excited to see each other and not annoyed like we often used to be.

The aeroplane safety instructions say to put your oxygen mask on before helping others in an emergency. Being a good parent and a good partner doesn't mean you always have to be by their sides. If you want space, you aren't failing in your duties. We don't have to be together twenty-four-seven as one happy nuclear family. When we cater to our specific needs, we're more capable of delivering world-class parenting. The calmer we are, the better parents we can be. If taking a break will help you be a better parent, then that really is the best thing you can do for yourself and your family – contrary to popular opinion.

And don't ever give your children drugs.

Chapter Seventeen

The Advocate

Prior to that day, I had never met someone with dwarfism. It was 3 November 2019 and I had been invited by Zoe, my podcast co-host and now very close friend, to speak on a panel about identity and purpose at her 'What Women Want' event. I arrived early, by request, for a VIP lunch that would kickstart the festivities. I had been promised a fancy meal, an even fancier goodie bag, and an introduction speech delivered by Zoe to her most influential attendees.

We had just finished co-hosting the first season of *The Baby Bubble*. My star was slowly rising, though I hadn't yet made a big name for myself in the parenting media landscape or spoken on a panel at an event like this, so my anxiety was high. 'You're not likely to know a single soul,' I said to myself in the parking lot. 'And you're one of only four men in attendance at an event with "women" in the title.'

I was concerned that I was infiltrating a sacred space, and it had taken every ounce of willpower to convince myself not to pretend I was ill and bail at the last minute. This was Zoe's event, and she was one of my most supportive friends, so I coached myself out of the car and towards the venue. When I walked in, sweat pouring from my armpits, I spotted a large, live macaw with its handler in the corner of the room, likely a hangover from the previous event. This put me strangely at ease, as I knew that the colourful bird would easily trump the gay dad in the crowd.

There were three groups of women, separated by a large black table covered in beautiful white flowers and mint-green bottles of Bellini Cipriani. One of the groups of women was busy setting the table and adding large white goodie bags to each of the seats. The other two groups seemed lost in conversation, each at opposite ends of the room. My social anxiety was skyrocketing at the thought of picking one group over the other, as the wrong move could have a detrimental effect on the evening's success. I made a quick decision to introduce myself to the group closest to the macaw.

I wasn't aware of Charli Kate Adams' celebrity back then. I didn't know that she and her husband, Cullen, had made names for themselves as two of the most vocal and well-known dwarfism advocates in the country. I didn't know that they had a combined reach of over 400k on Instagram alone, which meant they were staples – Charli specifically – at influencer events. I didn't know, as I approached the group, that they were parents to two gorgeous young girls. I just saw a bubbly blonde woman who stood at four feet and two inches tall. She wore beautiful gold slippers and a white romper, and her nails were painted white to match her outfit, which I appreciated.

She pulled her focus from the conversation and locked eyes with me, causing the other two women to turn in my direction. I had one chance to make a strong first impression. 'I was planning to be the flamboyant life of the party – then I walked in and saw this fucking bird. Which one of you invited him?'

The women laughed, genuine giggles and a snort, which placed me right at ease.

I politely introduced myself, and each woman introduced herself to me. I soon learned that Charli was a content creator, an advocate and a speaker, as well as a wife and a mum. After a few minutes of chatting, I pulled out my phone and followed her on Instagram.

Zoe tapped the side of her champagne flute and asked the guests to be seated. I searched for my name card and found that I was at the opposite end of the table from Charli. We vowed to keep in touch online.

★

Charli and I soon developed a supportive online relationship. We passionately engaged with each other's content, frequently chatting in our DMs about the brands we were both creating advertisements for on Instagram. A bit more than colleagues and a bit less than close friends, we had been in each other's lives for a year by the time Charli suggested we get the kids together for a playdate. Naturally, I didn't hesitate to say yes.

Our online relationship was such a constant in my life that I didn't think to prep my children in any way for who they were about to meet. 'We're going on a playdate with my friends,' I said to the twins. Cooper refused to look up from his drawing, but Stella raised her head and said, 'Cool,' with a smile.

That was that.

When we arrived at the play centre, I carried the twins to the front door, where Charli, Cullen and their two kids were standing. I placed Stella down in front of Charli. Uncharacteristically for my daughter, she remained speechless as Charli said hello and introduced her children. Charli's daughters each have a different form of dwarfism, but the four children – mine and hers – stood at the exact same height, so it was impossible for my three year olds to notice this particular difference between them. But as we walked into the play centre, Stella whispered to me, 'Why is that child allowed to be a mommy?'

I realised I had made a mistake. My comfort in meeting up with my beautiful new friends and their kids meant absolutely nothing as far as my children's understanding was concerned. I'd just expected, mistakenly, that somehow the twins would know how to handle this unique interaction, but it was their first experience meeting people with dwarfism, and naturally they wanted information from me.

Over the course of the two-hour playdate, Stella kept quietly asking me very understandable questions about Charli and Cullen. 'Are they adults like you?' 'Will I be taller than them soon?' 'How many adults look like them?' I was shocked, even though I should have expected this. Stella was a very inquisitive child who was obsessed with adults and asking them questions. Cooper on the other hand was much more interested in dinosaurs and slippery dips, so it wasn't surprising that he didn't ask a single question about Charli's family.

As an advocate, Charli often addressed these situations and questions with her audience, and I knew that she and Cullen could handle awkward whispers from young kids. But in these circumstances, should they have needed to? I hoped that any online friends of mine would explain my family structure – two dads, no mum – to their kids in advance of meeting us, yet I hadn't thought to do something similar.

I felt uncomfortable answering the questions while the twins and I were sitting right next to Charli and her family. I just kept whispering, 'That's a good question. We'll talk about it later.'

Each time I said this, I knew it was the wrong approach, but my mind couldn't commit to a plan. Maybe I could bring it up with Charli and politely request that she answer the questions … but would that make Stella uncomfortable? Would that make Charli uncomfortable? Maybe I could answer the questions directly at a normal volume … but would that make Charli's children uncomfortable? Maybe I could take the twins to the bathroom and answer Stella's questions in private … but would that make the topic seem worthy of secrecy or even shameful? There wasn't a perfect option, so I froze and chose to deal with it all later.

Charli and her family didn't seem to notice the back-and-forth I was having with Stella. But honestly, I wasn't sure. The kids got along brilliantly, and I had a fabulous time swapping influencer war stories with veterans of the game. We said our goodbyes, and everyone had massive smiles on their faces, but the lump in my throat made it hard for me to focus on anything other than the car ride home and how I'd approach the situation.

As soon as I pulled out of the parking lot, Stella began shooting rapid-fire questions at me. These weren't inappropriate by any means, and I felt I had a strong answer for each one. But the weight of my mistake hung heavy on my heart. It was possible that the Adamses hadn't noticed a single thing; that they were driving away commenting on how fabulous the playdate had been. But I felt that I had failed them as well as my children. Everything was new to the twins, and it was my job to help prepare them for the world as best I could and talk things through with them so they could be courteous to others. And I had dropped the ball.

After dwelling on my discomfort for far too long, I realised the only way to ease my anxiety was to do something about it. I was too nervous to have the conversation with Charli, thinking I could potentially make a 'nothing' situation into 'something'. But I knew I could – needed to, really – talk with my children. Stella and Cooper would come across people with dwarfism again – Charli and her family, of course, and surely others too. Plus, my kids would come across other people with all kinds of visible differences. I wanted to make sure this situation didn't happen again.

The following week, I put together a list that included people in wheelchairs, amputees, blind people, deaf people, and people with albinism, vitiligo, alopecia and cystic acne. Then I searched for relevant people with Instagram accounts I could follow. I googled 'vitiligo' and found Winnie Harlow, then 'albino' and found Shaun Ross, then 'wheelchair' and found Shane Burcaw, then did more searches and found many others. I sat the twins down and showed them the accounts – not all at once, of course. Sometimes the kids laughed; sometimes they explained that they'd already learned about this from Daddy.

At other times, we had conversations that I found very challenging. One of them took place when I showed my kids a YouTube video of Deepa Berar, a woman with alopecia.

'Why are you showing this to us?' Cooper asked.

'Because I want you to see all the different types of people in the world.'

'But why? We're not like that.'

*

It's hard for me to put into words what it feels like to grow up never coming across representations of people like you. Quite early on in their lives, my straight friends felt seen and heard and understood, knowing they had a place in the world. All the lyrics of their favourite songs, all the movies we watched and all the television shows we raced home from school to record featured love stories that matched the ones in their hearts. Sadly, I never had that feeling when I was a young boy. From the second I realised I was different, I began to search for that difference in the fictional worlds I could access – an example, any example, of someone like me. What I most wanted to find was a happy queer character, but I always came up empty-handed.

I was only four in 1993, when the movie *Philadelphia* broke down barriers by addressing the AIDS epidemic. I was five when *Priscilla Queen of the Desert* was released, six when *To Wong Foo* made its cinematic debut, and seven when *The Birdcage* arrived at my local theatre. But I was far too young to benefit from the impact of those diverse storylines gracing our screens.

Ellen DeGeneres came out as a lesbian on national television in 1997. I was eight, old enough to grasp the importance of the monumental news, but my parents didn't add it to the dinnertime communication agenda. Neither did my grandparents, nor my teachers, nor my friends at school. But maybe I was too distracted trading Pokémon cards to notice anyway.

Then I turned eleven. The year was 2000 and I was quite confident that I was – unless God had plans to switch things up after puberty – a homosexual. That was when the stoner comedy *Dude, Where's My Car?* hit the local theatre, and strangely my brother and I were allowed to see it. I found myself watching in astonishment as characters played by Ashton Kutcher and Seann William Scott swapped an aggressively sloppy kiss in an attempt to freak out Fabio, the famous body-building model, who was sitting in the car next to theirs at a stoplight. The film brushed the kiss off as a cheeky bromance moment, with the boys high-fiving for 'winning' against a disgusted Fabio, who sped away. My brother laughed, an understandable reaction for a ten year old. I laughed too. That was the first time I saw two boys kiss on the big screen.

I saw glimpses of myself – often caricatures – in other films and on TV. *Zoolander* was released a year later, a comedy film in which Mugatu, played by Will Ferrell, had a homoerotic relationship with his assistant. Bridget Jones had a gay best friend named Tom. The protagonist of *Clueless*, Cher, had a crush on a new boy at school who turned out to be gay. *Best in Show* had lesbian and gay characters. Miss New York was a lesbian in

Miss Congeniality. Damian from *Mean Girls* was gay. And who could forget the gay cheerleader, Les, in *Bring It On*? I certainly haven't.

On the big screen, people like me had small roles. In the media I could access, they were almost always the butt of a joke and never – ever – the romantic lead. But those characters gave me a glimmer of hope that there were others like me out there. As far as I could tell, there were at least a dozen of us in America.

Then I turned seventeen. The year was 2005 and I was working at the front counter of the Regal Cinema in Concord. I was out of the closet now, confident in myself, and surrounded by a wildly supportive group of employees and managers.

One night I was collecting my paycheque, reeking of buttered popcorn after a long shift, when my manager asked, 'Are you excited about *Brokeback Mountain*?'

'What's so exciting about Rattlesnake Mountain?' I replied, referencing a nearby mountain with beautiful hiking trails, where I'd often walked with my Boy Scout troop.

'No, the new movie where Jake Gyllenhaal and Heath Ledger's characters are gay.'

'Oh, yeah, of course,' I lied, not skipping a beat. 'I'm really excited about it. Who's the female lead again?'

'Michelle Williams!'

'Yeah, that's right. I just adore her.'

I immediately sent in a request to work opening night. I didn't want to be in the audience for that movie. It felt far too exposed, even though I was out of the closet and had a few good friends who would have gone with me. I didn't have any plot spoilers and wasn't sure how I'd react to what looked like a serious drama, as someone who is prone to sobbing hysterically when consuming emotional media. I wanted to sit back and observe the situation from afar.

On opening night, I was working the cash register, and a sense of pride began to overcome me as I printed out each ticket. It was our time, a movie for us. I only knew of a handful of openly gay men in Concord and the surrounding area, and they all – one by one by one by one – came strolling in with their fruit flies (a much more polite version of 'fag hag'). But they were far from the only ones: the session was sold out. Queers and allies alike were here to celebrate. A few employees had snuck in from the back with plans to watch part of the movie during their shift.

At the Regal, nearly all of the movies started around the same time, staggered just a few minutes apart. That meant the staff, especially the cash register duo, had a large chunk of time to relax and eat popcorn. Staff members would do movie checks, walking in shortly after each one began to ensure that the film was clear, the sound quality was good and the emergency exits were working. It wasn't my job to run the check for *Brokeback Mountain*, but I asked if I could do it.

I entered into the back of the dark theatre and stared at the aisle in front of me: it was packed with teenagers sitting on the floor. Normally I'd have asked each of them to return to their seat or leave the theatre, but that night I couldn't – I wouldn't. I walked slowly through the maze of teenagers staring at the screen, each with a smile on their face. When I got to the bottom of the aisle, I glanced at the emergency doors, barely taking my eyes off the screen, then made my way back up, my gaze now darting around to check each patron's face. Were they happy or disgusted? Young or old? Happy or sad?

At the top of the crowded aisle, I kneeled down to watch some of the movie. It wasn't a planned or professional move, but my body took over.

On the screen, nothing monumental was happening yet. The two leads were just herding sheep. But I noticed a young gay man, a few rows in front of me in an aisle seat, wiping tears from his eyes. He was from a neighbouring town. We knew each other vaguely, like passing ships in the sea of musical theatre performed around our state. Even though I should have been watching the movie, I couldn't keep my eyes off of him as I wondered why he was crying. They hadn't even kissed yet.

Then it hit me: he was smiling. Those tears he was wiping from his face were happy tears. They began to stream down my face too. I was in a packed cinema on the opening night of a global movie release, and for the first time in my young life I was watching two men fall in love on the big screen. Finally, here was a story that didn't require me to rewrite the narrative in my imagination so that I could relate to its premise.

When I returned to work ten minutes later, still wiping away tears, I got excited about seeing the audience pour out. How would they react?

After the credits rolled, I eavesdropped on the sea of straight people leaving the theatre. 'That was beautiful!' 'I'm so happy it was made!' 'I'll never forget that film.' 'That is going to win the Oscar for Best Picture.' 'We have to tell Brian and Mark to see that immediately.'

I watched the full movie a few days later, in a near-empty theatre at noon on a Tuesday. Then I watched it again on the Thursday night and on the Sunday evening, and again on the Monday morning. In many ways, it was like discovering a queer version of the Bible. The film was unapologetically gay. It was all ours – well, ours and theirs.

Every time I saw *Brokeback Mountain*, I was watching it with straight people. They benefited greatly from it too, because it offered them a glimpse into our lives, a peek behind a curtain into a place where they usually weren't invited. Through the power of that film, they gained empathy for queer love – hidden, secretive, difficult, but just as real as theirs.

★

'So why are we watching someone who isn't like us?' my son asked me.

'Well, when we see different types of people and watch stories about them, or meet people who are different from us, like when we met Charli and her family, then we're more likely to be kind to them and people like them. That makes the world a bit easier for them.'

'Should the world be easy?'

I gave him a soft smile. I thought back to my childhood and how wonderful it would have been to have considered it 'easy'. To have had access to technology and representation that made it possible for others to understand people like me better. I thought, as Cooper stared at me waiting for a response, just how relieved I was that he wouldn't have to deal with the same kind of thing. I took a deep breath, exhaled and spoke. 'That's a really good question. I think it's a goal worth fighting for, to try and make the world easier for everyone.'

'Easier for me?' he asked.

'Yes, easier for you.'

Chapter Eighteen

The Dad Bashing

A few years into my parenting journey, I went out with a group of women: five mothers, to be precise, all of whom I had met online. They were influencer mums, each with their own impressive followings and families.

I drove forty-five minutes out of the city to meet the ladies for dinner on a Thursday. I was running late, so they were already seated and halfway through their first round of cocktails when I arrived. We said our hellos, and they picked up their conversation: a comical dad-bashing session inspired by a few horror stories from the previous week. Three of the mothers were dragging their 'worthless' husbands through the parenting coals, while the other two mums remained silent, with giddy smiles on their faces.

'Dads are shit!' Mum #1 said with a laugh.

'All of them,' Mum #2 added.

'Not you, of course.' Mum #1 gestured in my direction. 'You don't count.'

'All of my girlfriends have the exact same problems, you know,' Mum #3 chimed in, inspiring the rest of the girls to nod. 'All of them. Always having to ask their husbands to do everything, always getting fifty per cent of their effort.'

'It's a bloody epidemic,' Mum #2 suggested, prompting the rest of the girls to laugh.

I was used to dad bashing by this point: I'd been working in the parenting media space for over a year and had become accustomed to reading, 'Hey, Dads, it's time to step it up!' headlines from even the more progressive of parenting media organisations. My rational brain understood the need for this level of venting, especially among close friends. The truth was, straight men did it too, behind their wives' backs: 'Wives are always complaining. Wives are never happy. Wives take everything too damn seriously!' I knew, in theory, that it was a healthy way of letting off steam and connecting with one another on a topic that was low-hanging fruit, a bit like talking about the weather. You knew exactly how everyone was going to respond, but it made you feel good to say it out loud.

When I first started hearing mums speak like this, I would take great offence. 'Not all men,' I'd reply. 'I know so many fantastic dads.' But that never sufficed, not once. Not only was it not empathetic, but they already knew that I knew they weren't, actually, talking about *all* men. That comment didn't add to the conversation in any way. And it certainly didn't make up for the actions of *some* men. Instead, it deflected from the issues at hand. Over time, I grew capable of nodding along and hearing these mothers out. I knew what they meant, and I learned how to support them. When mums said 'all dads' in front of me, I heard 'uninvolved cis straight fathers'. The types of men who deserved the negative press: the ones who forgot about anniversaries, who cheated, wouldn't do any chores, and were more interested in playing video games or golf with their mates than listening to how their wives' days were. The ones who looked nothing like me, my husband or my own dad.

*

I've always thought of my father as simply wonderful. On paper he's an all-American masculine man, but unlike the cowboys in famous Westerns, he has a modern sensibility that I didn't see in other fathers when I was growing up. Yes, he built and maintained our homes with an impressive collection of equipment rivalling that of professional construction workers. Sure, like the other local dads, he maintained our property, mowed the lawn and ensured that the chickens were well taken care of. But he also did the grocery shopping, took charge of the laundry, and did the dishes after my mother cooked. When she crafted, he purchased the items and tidied up. And when she had a project planned, like a garden bed, he brought her vision to life in twenty-four hours or less. Sure, he wasn't perfect – sometimes she needed to remind him of important events that he would have forgotten if it wasn't for her master calendar. But they were – and still are – an incredible duo.

Growing up, I knew that I had a strong example of modern manhood in my house. Dad encouraged us to cry, let us vent after breakups and taught us to fight with our words not our hands – okay, he also taught us how to fight with our hands, but

This is my favourite picture of me and Dad, standing in front of a New England backdrop with a long quahog (clam) rake in our hands.

it was words first. He did many of the things that my friends' moms did: he helped us with homework each night, he got us up out of bed and out the door each morning, he took charge of breakfasts because my mom owned dinners, and he never – not ever – missed a dance recital, a football game or a swim meet. Unlike his role models, the men who came before him in his long family tree, Dad told us frequently and showed us constantly that he loved us. He gave us big hugs, held our hands in public and kissed us on the forehead. He loved watching football and baseball, but he also liked romantic comedies, and he didn't sit on his ass watching TV with a beer in his hand like the dads in sitcoms.

'Lazy' or 'uninvolved' or 'lacking empathy' weren't words that applied to the man – he was 'active', 'hardworking' and 'energetic'. So when I got older, had kids and started hearing the 'lazy dad' trope thrown around, I thought, *Not my dad*. My dad was 'not like other dads' – I always knew that. And his determination to break the generational and cultural curse of uninvolved, emotionless men was a large part of what inspired me to be not like other dads too.

★

'Please tell me Josh is like this, too?' Mum #2 asked me as our dinner arrived.

'Um, he's really not,' I sheepishly responded. 'He's involved in every aspect.'

'So is my husband,' Mum #4 replied, giving me a relieved look.

'You found the only two unicorns in Australia, you lucky bitches,' said Mum #1, chugging the rest of her drink.

I didn't have the courage to share with these mothers that my husband was the definition of supportive. And I wouldn't dare tell them that my father and father-in-law were stand-up blokes, too As were many of our friends, like the singer Josh Pyke, my old boss Eric and writer Scott Stuart. It didn't matter that I could list a handful of stay-at-home fathers and other passionate dads who lost sleep each night while thinking about their children's happiness – the dads in most of these women's lives weren't like that, which meant that to them, any other example would just be 'a rare unicorn in a sea of shitty dads'. I started to wonder if maybe what these women actually meant when they said 'all dads are shit' was that their partners and their fathers were shit. If so, the 'all' was them desperately wishing that their struggles at home could be validated as 'normal'.

The 'shitty dad' conversation only took up the first twenty minutes of a lovely long dinner, but I couldn't get it out of my head. In fact, I had to excuse myself to the bathroom and splash my face with water. *This isn't an attack on you, brother – this is an attack on their partners*, I reminded myself. I returned to the table and suppressed my feelings.

That same week, I received an email from a popular news publication with a headline that made my blood boil all over again: yet another statement from a contributing writer that lumped 'all dads' together when, I believed, the writer was simply admitting that her husband wasn't pulling his own weight.

Because I couldn't get the topic out of my head, I called Zoe, my parenting partner in crime, in hopes of working through the issue out loud with a mother I really trusted – someone I knew I could be honest with, without fear of being cancelled.

'I don't understand what mothers think they're doing when they talk like this,' I told Zoe, feeling agitated. 'Do they genuinely believe that this "all dad" messaging is going to make a positive difference? How would you feel if you opened your email and read a headline that said something like, "Hey, mums! It's time you stopped being stressed-out clean freaks who prioritise your kids over yourselves"? Would you try to be less anxious or just get really annoyed, even angry?'

There was a silence on the other end of the phone, and I worried that I had overstepped. Just then, Zoe whispered, 'Fox, Mommy is on the phone with Uncle Sean. I'll help you in one minute.' I heard the faint sound of the television clicking on, then Zoe returned. 'Sorry, I'm here. I'm listening, keep going.'

'Until recently, this narrative that dads are shit was pretty damn true across the board. Domestic abuse was considered acceptable. Marital rape was legal. Women couldn't even own credit cards in their own names. Men just worked and didn't help with the kids – like, at all. That was "normal" for a very, very long time. But we've made massive strides in the right direction. The number of women working now is higher than ever before, and the average husband helps with his kids today. More dads are stepping their shit up. Parenting responsibilities have started to be more evenly shared.'

'Well, not all couples share responsibilities evenly,' Zoe chimed in.

'True. I just don't believe anyone really believes that, in today's landscape, *all* dads are shit. Why not just say what we know you're really thinking, Barbara? You have a shitty husband – your kids have a shitty-ass dad.'

Zoe was laughing. She knew I was being melodramatic to add comedic flare to a serious topic. Clearly, despite my best efforts, I was still feeling personally victimised by the 'all dads' messaging and needed to let out my feelings in a safe space.

I was a great dad married to a great dad, and we'd been raised by great dads. I put so much damn effort into the gig that I felt, maybe irrationally, I wasn't getting the credit I was due when 'all dads' were slammed. No matter how much my friends reassured me that Josh and I didn't count because we were gay, I felt as though a bunch of terribly rotten apples were tainting our good name.

'I just don't understand what these women want,' I said. 'What do you think it is?'

'To feel heard – to feel seen,' Zoe replied without skipping a beat.

'So it's not about making things better?'

'Of course it is. They want that, but they don't know how to get it. They've tried, Sean. They've had discussions with their husbands, they've asked for more, they've reminded them and set up calendar invites and made lists, and they've complained again and again. But many of their partners, these "bad" dads, don't have the tools to do better and sometimes are resistant to seeking them out. It's a vicious cycle of women wanting more, complaining about it, not getting it, and then going home to experience it all over again.'

'But why complain, as a collective group, without wanting to work together to make it all better? I just wonder what would happen if these mothers replaced "all" with "my". If they addressed the elephant in the room.'

'I don't think those women would ever do that,' Zoe replied. 'It would be too humiliating for them. And lord knows, men don't usually respond well to being shamed. Plus, some of these mums care a lot about not being perceived as "a difficult woman" – and that's understandable. I think "all" is less of a personal attack on their husbands and more of an observation on the way our society tends to ignore the efforts of mothers while praising fathers for doing the bare minimum.'

'I can get behind that,' I said, finding her insights very helpful.

'And I wonder … maybe it's actually working? Maybe this messaging has, little by little, changed the way we parent. Mums are more empowered to speak up online, and dads are less able to avoid their responsibilities. Maybe the thing that's bugging you is actually making the parenting space better in a lot of ways.'

'Yeah, good point,' I conceded. 'I'm worried, though, that the men who most need to hear this message aren't in the right spaces. These dads aren't reading the Babyology headlines like I am or devouring *This Glorious Mess* podcasts each week like I do. The "all dads" messaging is actually for mums much more than it is for dads – it's for mothers to bond with each other in adversity. And as a gay man and a parenting media personality, I just so happen – oh shit, this is a big insight – to be welcomed into the spaces where this messaging is being widely used. I shouldn't be asking for a seat and then judging everyone else at the table. That's not fair.'

'This is huge, Sean. What happens next?' Zoe was not a friend I called simply to complain – after talking about an issue, we'd always discuss potential solutions.

'I guess I've just figured out that I'm not stuck in the middle of the parenting world – I can chat with the dads, and I'm welcomed into private conversations with the mums. But I'm unsatisfied with the conversations being held behind closed doors about both mums and dads. And because I'm a father, I've focused on being unsatisfied with what's being said about dads.'

'Then maybe you could do something about that.'

This was the motivation I needed. Right after we ended the call, I began writing a pitch for a unique podcast called *The Dad Kit*. I planned to interview famous Australian dads, in hopes of attracting the largest possible audience for the show. I wanted to figure out what was going on in the minds of modern fathers, so I searched for an eclectic bunch of men of various ages, sexualities and cultural backgrounds. This would be my chance, I hoped, to help shift the narrative about what a good dad really looked like.

Chapter Nineteen

The Wizard Of Oz

It was 10 am on 24 July and I'd been updating my Halloween Pinterest board for two entire hours. I hadn't planned on dedicating such a large chunk of my morning to this completely unnecessary task, especially when I was supposed to be watching my kids, but I'd got it in my head that I had no other choice. I told myself that if I was going to win Halloween this year, then I needed to get extremely serious about planning. Aggressively scrolling Pinterest and short-listing potential costumes for my family seemed like the perfect place to start.

I know that thinking about Halloween in July might seem ridiculous to some people – especially those parents who scurry back and forth between Big W and Kmart an hour before trick-or-treating begins, arm wrestling fellow last-minute shoppers for Elsa dresses that are two sizes too big. But it's right on schedule for me: I'm a proud homosexual father who considers Halloween to be the most important day of the calendar year.

Our twins were three months away from turning four, the age when they could finally appreciate Halloween. The foggy haze of the troubling first few years of parenthood had finally lifted, and I'd rediscovered my pre-parenting enthusiasm for life. I had friends to vent to about the challenges of being a dad, a therapy schedule that kept me grounded, and a few jobs that I absolutely loved. Plus, I had a wonderful husband who was just as excited about the baby years being over as I was.

Stella and Cooper were old enough to be enthusiastic about selecting their Halloween costumes, and young enough not to be totally embarrassed by me demanding that we dress to a pre-approved family theme. I was hyper-conscious that this agreeable holiday-participation window would be tiny. Any second now, my children would be rolling their eyes at the thought of me scheduling costume fittings and makeup tests in early September for a celebration that the rest of Australia would never fully appreciate – or not to my American standards, at least.

So I was enthusiastically wading in a puddle of holiday bliss. It was all part of my master plan to ensure Stella and Cooper fell madly, deeply and borderline inappropriately in love with Halloween.

*

My obsession with Halloween began when I was nine. It's seared into my memory like the scar on my right kneecap, the one I got on a hot summer day when I couldn't press the scooter brake because I was barefoot. That year I decided I wanted to be a toilet for Halloween. Let me repeat that: I wanted to be a toilet.

Because Mom and Dad practised the parenting philosophy of 'Sure, why the hell not?', they set out to turn me into the best toilet our town had ever seen – of course, the town had probably never seen a human dressed up as a toilet before. My parents didn't half-ass things: they were those annoying people who could make absolutely anything using just their hands, some tools and craft supplies, and a bit of imagination. First, Dad cut a hole in the top of a large packing box for my head to fit through. Then, on either side, he cut holes for my arms. Using glue, he attached a smaller packing box to the front, then he cut a hole where the toilet bowl would sit. We rushed off to Home Depot, and he purchased an actual toilet seat and a flush handle, which he attached to the boxes. He then painted the entire thing white. He added a pillowcase where the toilet bowl hole sat, so when I walked around on Halloween night I could simply lift up the seat for neighbours to throw in their candy.

That night I felt the euphoria of being supported. My idea was, arguably, ridiculous, and it was different from all the rest. The other kids dressed up as Ninja Turtles or Power Rangers, inexpensive costumes easily purchased from the local Walmart, but my parents – who could have just said 'no' or carefully manipulated me down a different path – gave themselves entirely to my idea, making my dream costume a reality.

As I walked around my neighbourhood, I received an endless stream of compliments. I felt on top of the world, like I had actually won Halloween. There I was at nine years old, being complimented by adults for doing something different, and I'd only played a tiny part in bringing this unique vision to life.

Without further ado, I give you the infamous toilet-seat costume. (Steven is the wizard and Samantha is the pirate.)

The experience planted a little seed of an idea in my head: *Being yourself and doing your own thing are worthy of celebration.* And it planted another seed in the same pot: *Your parents are supportive.* Mom and Dad had made me feel like I was part of a team and that my opinions were valid. Like any other kid, I was used to being told what to eat and where to go and what to wear. But that Halloween, I was a human being who could play a role in how I presented myself. From then on, I found it easier to include my parents in my 'unique' ideas, and I felt more comfortable being and expressing myself around everyone.

The toilet costume opened a creative door for me, becoming the origin story of many of the costumes and imaginative ventures that followed. These included the dresses and feather boas I put on as I paraded around my cousin's house, the wigs I wore as I performed scenes from *Annie* for my family, and the tabletop I decorated with a collage. Whenever I had a creative idea, my parents helped me bring it to life, teaching me that anything was possible: all I needed was a bit of imagination and a parent to drive me to Home Depot.

★

Just then, the 'Are you still watching?' prompt popped up on my television, rudely disrupting my Halloween Pinterest binge. My children, who had been locked in a *Bluey* trance, began screaming incoherently at the top of their lungs: '*Bluey*! Stop! More! Now!'

It seemed like as good of a time as any to begin parenting for the day, so I turned off the television and put on some pants.

'Who wants a mango smoothie?' I cheerfully sang as I opened the curtains to the outside world.

'Fine!' the twins replied, still looking annoyed that they wouldn't get to watch a fifty-seventh episode of their beloved *Bluey*.

'And how about we play some board games?' I added, skipping out of the room.

I did this often: I would ignore my parenting responsibilities for an hour or two, feel really shit about it and then dive head-first into the role of Perfect Dad, brimming with recipe ideas and crafting projects. I was, at my very best, a lot like Martha Stewart – you know, without a vagina or jail time. Because of my parents, I could sew, paint and draw just about anything if looking at a reference. And when you pair that with a stubbornness that convinces me I can achieve greatness with a pair of scissors and some glue, I'm a pretty fun dad to be stuck in the house with.

'I have a question for you two,' I said to Stella and Cooper, as I sat on the floor among the board-game pieces that the twins had been chewing on while I made their smoothies.

'Yes, I wiped my hands after I pooped,' my son announced with confidence.

'No, no, no, not *that* question. But I am very proud of you.' I smiled. 'My question is: if you could dress up as anything for Halloween this year, what would you want to be?'

Stella stared up at the ceiling and tickled her chin. She had recently started mirroring me and Josh, and her adorable gesture was a sign that she was taking this seriously.

'We just need to make sure,' I said, 'that all four of us can do something together. You know, like a group or a team. The

Wiggles are a good example of a team – and there's four of them and four of us!'

'I want to be Dorothy!' Stella chimed in. 'With red heels!'

'Dorothy the Dinosaur from the Wiggles?'

'No, Dorothy with Toto!'

'And I will be the Cowardly Lion!' Cooper added, following up his unnecessarily loud comment with a boisterous 'ROARRRRR!'

According to Google, the twins were too young to watch *The Wizard of Oz*. But they were being raised by a musical theatre-loving homosexual, so the parenting rulebook had already flown out the window. I had put them on a healthy diet of Judy Garland and Julie Andrews films as soon as they could sit up and watch the television.

I was excited about the potential of a *Wizard of Oz* theme, so I abandoned setting up the board game, downed the final bits of my smoothie and typed 'Family Wizard of Oz Halloween Costumes' into Pinterest. Instantly I found some references to show the twins. 'Look, I could be the Tin Man and Daddy could be the Scarecrow,' I said, turning my iPad to show Stella and Cooper.

'I can have a dog in a basket.' Stella leaped to her feet, pointing to a picture on my screen of what looked like a real cat shoved into an orange trick-or-treat pumpkin basket.

'I can be the COWARDLY LION!' Cooper repeated, shaking with excitement.

'Then it's sorted.' I grinned at them. 'We're doing *The Wizard of Oz* this year!'

★

It was 2011, my very first Halloween in New York City. Josh and I were dressed as jailbait in matching orange jumpsuits, with black eyes and teardrop tattoos that I drew on with a six-dollar makeup kit. We started out at a few straight bars with our good friend James, and it was as terrible as you'd imagine: they were playing 'The Monster Mash' on repeat, and half the patrons weren't dressed up. I got 'Isn't Halloween for children?' vibes, which I took as a homophobic attack, and demanded we leave. We headed to Hell's Kitchen, where we stopped in at the Flaming Saddles saloon to visit my friend Kris.

It was there that I saw him. This wasn't just any old man dressed as a toilet: this was a not-so-old twink dressed as a *slutty* toilet.

The costume itself wasn't risqué: a stock-standard silver polyester slip with a foam base. But the twink had decided – brilliantly, I might add – to cut out holes and tape miniature red toy plungers on both nipples. The pièce de résistance was that he'd tucked the fabric into his underwear, a tiny thong decorated with toilet paper. It was, arguably, the best slutty toilet Halloween costume I had ever seen.

A half-hour later, I happened to be in the bathroom with the twink and a few other patrons. 'Are you a toilet?' a Pikachu asked while fixing his hair in the mirror.

'A throne. A crapper. A stool. Whatever tickles your fancy, my dear.' The twink shook off the final bits of his urinal wee.

'So why a toilet?' I asked, smiling sheepishly. I was hoping his response would allow me to share my childhood toilet story and bond with him – and then, naturally, we'd become good friends.

The twink turned from the mirror to face me before he walked my way. He placed a hand on my head as if to say, 'Pay attention, my child, class is in session', leaned forward and whispered, 'Because I fucking wanted to.' With a smile and a wink, he strode promptly out of the loo.

Minus the crass language and the cheeky antics, his answer had the same energy that my parents had gifted me all those years ago: *If you want to do something, you do it. If you have an idea, bring it to life. Don't do it for others, just trust your gut and bring your vision to the streets.*

As Josh and I went to the next club, Industry Bar, I saw a lot of queer people walking around Hell's Kitchen. There were gay and bi men in heels, drag queens and kings, and gender diverse people, all expressing themselves in bold and innovative ways: nudity, grunge, camp and horror. What they had in common was the genuine joy brought on by unbridled creativity. There wasn't a simple, off-the-rack costume in sight.

It was at Industry Bar that I first heard the queer name for Halloween. A drag queen hosting the night's performances was up on stage and said, 'Happy Gay Christmas! Today's our day. Halloween is our mother-fucking holiday. The straights have Christmas and Easter, and all that religious nonsense. But we … we get Halloween!'

When the crowd erupted all around me and Josh, we couldn't help but join in.

The moment felt powerful. I was surrounded by fellow queer people, each and every one of us dressed to the nines. Unlike at the straight bars from earlier in the night, no one at Industry Bar had half-assed looks. Eyebrows were blocked out to create alien faces, hair was bleached, and elaborate artworks were painted on. These people had dressed up exactly as they wanted, executing their creative ideas just like my father had for me when I was seven.

It started to click, right there in the bar: Halloween had always been a safe space for queer people. In the past we were forced to wear masks year-round to fit in, costumes that hid our flamboyant truth. On Halloween, the one day a year when it was socially acceptable to dress any way you'd like, there was no more hiding. For kids of my generation, it was the one day a year when we could comfortably explore gender and sexuality without fear of getting bashed or made fun of. For so many patrons of the gay bars I attended that night, Halloween was the light at the end of the tunnel. It may have been that wearing a feather boa or kitten heels around their neighbourhood had provided the glimmer of hope that kept them alive.

I overheard a trans woman say, 'All of my firsts were on Halloween. My first pair of heels, my first wig, my first attempt at a full face of makeup. I guess I lost my girl virginity on Halloween, too. I owe Halloween my life.'

That very same night, I learned that Halloween used to be the only day each year when American police wouldn't arrest people for cross-dressing.

I'd always known Halloween was special, but on that night in New York City, I realised it was so much more than a holiday for queer people: it was a way of life.

Our final stop of the night was The Ritz, the club where Josh and I had met only a few months earlier. He drank with his friends while I danced by myself, soaking up the magic of the night. I knew then, as the orange-and-black confetti fell from the sky, that I would never be the same. Halloween was my holiday – our holiday – and I was never going to forget it.

★

When our *Wizard of Oz* costumes finally arrived, the twins rushed to try them on. Cooper's Cowardly Lion costume fit like a glove. He squealed with excitement as I adjusted the ears and velcroed on the paws. He refused to take it off, running around the house singing 'If I Were King of the Forest'. Stella laid her entire outfit on the living-room rug: the ruby-red slippers, the blue-and-white gingham dress, the wicker basket and the hair bows. She inspected the look for a good ten minutes, circling it like it was her prey.

Then she asked, 'Can I try it on, Dada?'

'Yes, of course you can, sweetie.'

She grabbed my face with excitement. 'Can I try it on right now?'

'Yes, of course you can, sweetie!' I laughed.

The dress was almost perfect, with just a tad too much space around the waist. In every other household around Australia, it would have been considered absolutely fine.

But Stella wasn't satisfied. 'I think it's a bit too big.'

'That's why we do a fitting, to make sure you feel comfortable. And if you don't, then we fix it.'

'I don't like it.' She stared at the floor and grabbed at the excess fabric.

I winked. 'Then we'll fix it.' I pinched the back of the dress, right around the zipper; just enough so she felt a change while leaving room for her to move. 'How's this?'

'Perfect!'

We moved on to the shoes. They fit, but she was really struggling to walk in them.

'This is hard, Dada,' she said as she held on to the edge of our piano.

'We can practise a little each day, or we can get your flats and rhinestone–'

'Practice!' She wobbled across the room. 'No doggie?' she added, noticing that the basket was empty.

'Not yet. But we have time. We can buy one, if you'd like.'

'Toto is grey,' Cooper said helpfully. 'You can get a grey dog.'

'I want it to be a purple dog.'

'Toto isn't purple, Stella – Toto is grey.'

Cooper wasn't wrong, but I had a rule when it came to Halloween, the same one my parents had when they brought my toilet vision to life: the 'Sure, why the hell not?' rule.

'If Stella wants a purple dog,' I explained to Cooper, 'then Stella can have a purple dog. There aren't any rules. Halloween is only about having fun.' I turned to Stella and smiled. 'You're in control, baby girl. You tell me what dog you want, and we'll go find one.'

My daughter ended up picking the purple dog of her dreams.

A few days before Halloween, she noticed that Dorothy had white socks and begged me to get her matching ones. We ran around to find a pair at the last minute – it took four different shops, but we finally got ones she approved of.

I was really proud of myself that Halloween. I'd passed along the family tradition of taking the celebration seriously, and I'd encouraged and supported my twins in bringing their costume fantasies to life. And I had planted a seed in their heads that creativity was to be celebrated, childhood was about play, and Halloween could be the most spectacular holiday of the calendar year. Or should I say, Gay Christmas.

Have you ever seen a more adorable photo of a family skipping down the street on Halloween dressed as the cast of *The Wizard of Oz* during a global pandemic?

Chapter Twenty

The Question

I had a recurring dream for years after I found out we were having twins.

In a brownstone apartment in Brooklyn, I was sitting alone on my living-room floor, hand-sewing a fringe onto a flapper dress for my daughter's Halloween costume. It was a warm-ish October day, so the windows and the front door were open. There were lit candles on the coffee table, a calming technique I'd learnt to deploy when I needed to meet a tight deadline. I could hear children passing by the front of the house, rushing home after school to greet their sleep-deprived parents.

In the dream — or maybe it's a nightmare — the sweet sounds of Amos Lee's 'Sweet Pea' were quickly replaced with the painful cries of my daughter, who came running up the front steps with her brother and then leaped into my arms. I couldn't see her face, but her words were clear: 'The girls at school say I'm less of a woman because I don't have a real mom!' She kept repeating this until I woke up.

The Question

I didn't need a therapy session in order to decipher the nightmare. I had always been concerned about the damage I might cause my children by bringing them into this world without a mother. No matter how much work I did on myself, it always remained in the back of my head: a nagging, persistent fear that I'd set them up for failure.

And even though I believed that Josh and I were perfectly suited to parenthood, I worried that Stella and Cooper were less likely to have a childhood free of bullying than kids with both a mother and father.

★

As a gay kid who grew up in the 1990s, I understand – probably more than most adults – just how damaging a pack of nasty bullies can be.

Each school morning, my anxiety hit the second my eyes opened. I covered my face with a pillow, wondering if my parents would pretend to believe in another faked illness. In the shower, I saw the bullies' faces. While I got dressed, I mapped out my schedule and began preparing for the moments our paths might cross. While I ate breakfast, I repeated their potential insults in my head, rehearsing my responses and critically analysing their weaknesses. While I waited for the bus, I wished I'd worn a 'straighter' outfit or had different hair or had never tap danced at the school assembly in 6th Grade. After climbing onto the bus, I sank deep into my front-row seat, as far from the cool kids at the back as possible. I hoped and prayed that I would just be left alone.

At school, my heart raced faster and faster as I darted through the entrance, desperately searching for a familiar face: Sarah, Brittany or Rebecca. I clung to their sides for support. I hugged walls as I walked to class, avoided carrying books that could be knocked over and steered clear of large groups whenever possible. I was known to take long, complicated routes to single toilets in efforts to avoid being alone with one of the boys. I visited the nurses – oh, the refuge they provided – as often as I could.

When we had classes together, my bullies and I, I did my best to remain quiet. *If I keep my gay voice hidden*, I thought, *maybe they'll leave me alone today.* Whenever I was forced to speak in class, I deepened my voice as much as possible, replicating the sounds that naturally fell from my father's mouth. If the bullies looked my way, even just for a second, I kept my gaze to the ground for the rest of the class. If they spoke to me, I replied with short sentences to avoid any potential minefields.

A simple question like 'Are you gay?', asked for the forty-first time, would haunt me for days. I'd beat myself up for my timid 'no' and my painfully incriminating 'leave me alone'. I'd consider his face, his body language, and the crew surrounding him, and wonder why no one had stood up for me. I had missed another opportunity to put him in his place, replaying the scenario in my head in hopes of nailing it the next time. I'd rethink and aggressively plan and work myself up to another painful anxiety attack, at the hands of a prepubescent teen filled with hate.

This, my friends, was just the first week of school.

The recurring nightmares yanked my childhood trauma into a salad bowl of fear and shame around my decision to raise kids without a mother. But the nightmares persisted long after the twins were born, when I'd started gaining confidence in my ability to parent well – not just well, fabulously. But although I knew that Josh and I were excellent fathers, would the rest of the world ever agree? I was consumed with fear that other adults would derail the great work my husband and I were doing at home.

★

I was picking up clothes from a local laundromat with Stella and Cooper, when they were three and a half. The attendant, a nice Asian woman in her fifties, offered them Fruity Chews from her lolly bowl. 'One for you, one for you, one for Daddy and one to take home to Mummy.'

Cooper was oblivious to the suggestion, reaching deep into the bowl to grab his chew and leaving Stella – in true gentleman's fashion – to handle the request by herself. But she was confused. She looked up at me, then back at the woman to await further instructions.

'Which one will Mummy like?' the attendant asked. 'Take one for Mummy.'

'One for Daddy?' Stella timidly asked as she grabbed one for Josh.

'Daddy already has one. Mummy needs one, too.'

I had recently decided – poor timing, I know – that it was important to let the twins work through some of their issues by themselves. I was prone to diving in and attempting to fix a problem before giving them a chance to solve it, a complex

I was addressing with my therapist. I wanted to step back and wait for Stella to ask me for help. But right on cue, she looked up at me again with eyes that screamed, 'Please, help!'

I dove in. 'Stella and Cooper have two daddies,' I said, smiling.

'No mummy?' the woman asked politely.

'That's right, no mummy.'

'Where is mummy?' she asked me, looking genuinely perplexed.

'They don't have a mummy,' I said, slowing down this time and starting to get a bit irritated. 'They have two dads. Some children have two dads.'

'Oh no, little girls need mummy.' She looked sad.

We had already paid for the clothes, and I could feel the frustration – and maybe the tears – building up inside of me.

I was supposed to be prepared for this. I had even role-played situations like this with Josh prior to the twins being born. But I had never planned on someone pushing back after I'd kindly articulated our situation – especially in front of my obviously uncomfortable children.

So I did what any anxious parent would have done: I thanked her, grabbed the basket of clothes and whisked the children out the front door in ten seconds flat.

At the car I buckled Cooper in first and then made my way over to address the situation with Stella. 'Are you okay?' I asked.

She deployed her new favourite comeback: 'Why do you ask?'

'Was that woman making you a little uncomfortable?'

'She kept saying "mummy, mummy, mummy" all of the time.'

'That's right, she did. Do you understand why she kept saying that?'

'Because she wants me to have a mummy.'

'You know that most children do have a mummy, right?'

Stella nodded. 'Yes.'

'Some people forget that not everyone does. Maybe she hadn't met an amazing kid like you with two daddies yet – maybe it's new to her.'

'I want a mummy,' she said, looking me directly in the eye.

Stella was deflated, and honestly, so was I. She dropped her chin to her chest and began biting her nails.

'I understand, sweetie.' I gently cupped her chin, and she looked up at me again. 'It's okay that you feel that way. You can always tell me about it and I will always listen to you.'

Stella nodded, tilting her head away from my hand.

'Just know that Daddy and Dada love you very much. And some people don't have a dad. Everyone's a little bit different, and different is …?'

'Beautiful,' she said, rolling her eyes.

Encounters like that one in the laundromat are why, I imagine, the nightmare persisted. No matter how hard I worked to rewire my brain, the world would step in, completely unannounced, and play the role of childhood bully. Strangers planted seeds of doubt in my children's minds. What could I do to prevent that?

Not long after, I took the kids to a playground. I was minding Cooper, who belly-surfed down a slide on repeat, while Stella played with a soccer ball that had been left unattended. A Russian woman, maybe in her late thirties, was pushing her baby in a swing nearby and having a very noisy phone chat with another Russian woman on loudspeaker.

Stella's ball must have rolled near her or something, because they began talking. I kept my focus on Cooper but watched out of the corner of my eye as I listened in.

'I love your hair!' the woman offered kindly.

'Thank you,' said Stella.

'Did your mum do your hair?'

Stella pointed in my direction. 'No, Dada.'

I smiled and waved at the woman, who looked my way but refused to smile back. 'Mum taught him well.'

'I have a dada and a daddy.'

'Well, everyone has a mummy.'

I rushed to Stella's side. 'Excuse me. She is three years old. She doesn't have a mum. Being a mum is more than just giving birth – it's a title that's earned.'

I scowled at the woman, scooping Stella off the ground and screaming to Cooper that it was time to go. I marched out of the park, holding back tears, and shoved everything, my children included, into the car.

We sat in silence for a couple of minutes while I calmed myself down.

'Does everyone have a mummy?' Stella said after a few minutes.

'No, sweetie. That woman was wrong. Everyone is born from a woman, but that doesn't make that woman a mother. I didn't give birth to you or give you my little seeds, but I'm still your dad. It's a title that's earned.'

But I wasn't sure if the message was getting through to her and Cooper. We were having open and honest conversations about our family at home, but our precious little humans were just toddlers: issues like infertility and queerphobia were way beyond their developmental capabilities. They knew most children had a mother and a father. They knew who had carried them and who had offered her eggs. They didn't believe – not even for a second – that it was wrong to have a family like ours. We wouldn't allow it. But outside our home, people like these women brought their negative reactions into our children's lives.

Josh was blunter than me. Once, at an airport security checkpoint, a staffer kept peppering us with a question: 'Where is Mummy? Aww, poor kiddies, where is Mummy?' Josh turned to him and said, cheerfully, 'She died.' That shut him right up.

Whenever I complained to my nearest and dearest, they said things like, 'It's fine. It's not that big of a deal. Don't worry, the kids won't remember it.'

But I remembered it – all of it. My parents would tell me that no matter what other kids said, I was perfect just the way I was, and that God loved me. But when the bullies repeatedly said otherwise, I questioned if my parents were telling the truth. How could I believe them? They had to say these nice things to make me feel better. It was the opinions of bullies that really started to matter to me, because those kids weren't being forced to pretend I was normal. If they said I was a sinner or a freak, then maybe I actually was.

As an adult, I was still having nightmares because of people like this. When a strange adult told my children that they needed a mother, what was stopping Stella and Cooper from believing

Stella wanted flowers painted on her face that day. I watched a dozen YouTube tutorials, spent $120 on makeup and held an impromptu photoshoot. Anything for my girl.

it? And if they started to believe that having a mum was the only way to be 'normal' and that 'normal' meant 'happy', then they might start thinking of their lives as sad. That, from personal experience, is a truly damaging way to grow up.

I pretended I was fine. I wrote articles and Instagram posts read by thousands of Australian parents, making them think I had all the confidence in the world in raising my boy and girl twins as a gay father. But deep down I felt I had – much like with climate change – brought my kids into a world destined to be shit for them.

★

After day care pick-up, we would sometimes stop at a nearby park and play for an hour before heading home. The twins had turned four, and Stella had met a new girl at day care, one of the older kids who was off to kindergarten soon. She suggested we play at the park together. For the sake of this story, her name was Penelope★.

While Penelope played with Stella and Cooper, I got to talking to her mother. We discovered that we lived on the same street, just a few houses apart. We both worked in creative fields, were from other countries, and did school drop-offs and pick-ups while our husbands were at the office. It was the middle of the pandemic, so we were chatting from across a bench and through masks, but the chemistry was strong and the dialogue flowed swimmingly.

When we all exited the playground and walked onto the footpath home, Penelope turned to Stella and asked, 'Where's your mummy?'

Penelope's mother and I were walking a few steps behind as the words fell from the girl's mouth. Her mother stopped talking in the middle of a sentence. I could feel her heart stop and her eyeballs bulge out of her face.

'I don't have a mummy,' Stella replied. 'I have two dads.'

Cooper jumped straight in. 'We have one daddy and one dada!'

Penelope's mother turned to me. 'Oh my god, I'm so sorry. I swear we've spoken about this with h–'

'Please don't be sorry! It's totally fine – they're all just learning.'

But Penelope looked sad, so we stopped walking. She turned to Stella and said, 'I really wish I could have two daddies.'

I watched as massive smiles grew on the faces of Stella and Cooper. I'll never know exactly what they were thinking, but I like to believe it was pride. Someone else, a new friend, wanted exactly what they had.

Penelope's mum responded like an absolute champion. 'You remember that sometimes people have a mum and a dad, and sometimes they don't? Well, Stella and Cooper have two dads, and Lilly★ from gymnastics has two mums, and Bryce★ just has one mum. Everyone's families are a little bit different. Does that make sense?'

Before Penelope could respond, Cooper jumped in. 'Yes, it does!'

It took that simple encounter to give me hope for the future. I'd been dragging the past into the present without considering how much the circumstances had changed. Stella and Cooper weren't growing up in the 90s in small-town USA. Sure, bullies would still be mean, and random adults would still be queerphobic; we'd have to work through those issues together as a family. But my kids had something I never did: examples of happy people, all around us, living very similar lives to ours. Stella and Cooper wouldn't have to look far to see themselves reflected in the world. My kids were growing up in a time and place where infertility was discussed openly, marriage equality was legal, rainbow families could more easily have kids, and queer characters weren't just the butt of jokes in pop culture but romantic leads in mainstream coming-of-age films and TV shows. My kids had hope.

I don't have that recurring dream anymore. Although I'd like to think it's because I'm much more confident today in how I'd respond if that nightmare scenario happened, I know it's actually because of a little girl and her mum, who gave me hope for a better future.

Chapter Twenty-one

The Queen

I knew I wasn't supposed to show it to the kids. If conservative politicians and religious leaders were correct, this three-minute YouTube video could cause irrevocable damage. Cooper might decide it was acceptable for boys to play dress-ups, paint their nails and even dance around the living room singing at the top of their lungs. Stella might wake up the next morning screaming, 'Yass, queen!' or 'Sashay away!' My twins might be accepting of queer people and feel comfortable expressing themselves authentically in front of their father and me. Who would be friends with children like them? And how would they process the trauma?

But I couldn't help myself: I had to share my love of drag queens with my children.

Around the time I turned eighteen, in 2006, I found out from a friend of a friend that there was an 'Under 21 Night' at one of the few gay bars in the state of New Hampshire: Club 313. I desperately wanted to kiss someone who was, like me, out of the closet. Just a few short months away from college, I needed to make sure I arrived on campus with more gay experience. So I peer-pressured my best friend Sarah into driving us there.

That night was the first time I saw a drag queen in the flesh. She was a red-headed plus-size queen with terribly blended makeup that stopped right above her Adam's apple, revealing the top of a breast plate that didn't match her skin colour. Her eyebrows weren't covered properly, so it looked like she had two sets. Her wig was best described as crunchy, her dress was three or four sizes too big, and she walked around the club as if she'd never once taken a step in heels before. Sarah and I didn't know her name, so just between us we referred to her as 'Trainwreck'.

I was, as you can probably tell from that judgemental admission, a teenage twat. I knew absolutely nothing about the art form of drag and had no experience with makeup or costuming outside of theatre. But I instantly became a qualified judge – as gay men often feel is our God-given right – turning to my friend and mocking the queen behind her back: 'Doesn't she own a brush?' 'Where did she learn to do makeup, Walmart?' 'Should I offer to take that dress in for her? Or better yet, *take it* and throw it *in* the garbage?'

I was a bratty teenager with so much internalised homophobia rushing through my veins that I used cheap comedy to mask my discomfort. The truth was, I was jealous: not of her drag – I didn't have an interest in getting dressed up like that – but of her confidence. I watched as she flirted with boys and enjoyed drinks purchased by older patrons. She spoke loudly, each self-deprecating sentence funnier than the last. She filled the space with her presence, commanding attention with every move. I found it impossible to look away.

She was seemingly unaware of her flaws, or at least wasn't held back by them. I later realised I wasn't sure if the dodgy makeup and dry wig were part of her character. Whatever her intentions, by golly her act worked. Every minute, without fail, she had a new dollar bill in her hand – sometimes fives, sometimes twenties. The joke was absolutely on me.

At that time in my life, I was consumed by what I saw as my flaws. The potential criticism of others, especially in relation to my sexuality, was playing on a loop in my head. I avoided clothes that seemed 'too gay' and reserved my true campiness for close friends. Dressing femme, walking femme, wearing femme jewellery or, god forbid, a wig – even just for fun – was drawing attention to the one thing I was hoping to hide.

But that drag queen wasn't held back by those fears – not in Club 313, at least. I assumed that underneath her ill-fitting dress, she was a gay man like me, but this gay man wasn't afraid to mess up or be laughed at. This gay man got up on that stage in front of a hundred or so local queers and brilliantly performed Spice Girls songs. I didn't know the terminology back then, but she 'gave good mouth', meaning she lip-synced so well it looked as if she was singing live. The spark inside of her, that drive to perform and make people laugh, radiated around the room. It was spectacular.

And just like that, in under an hour, I dropped my judgement of drag queens.

★

I decided to introduce my children to drag because of an interview I did with Marc Fennell on my new Spotify podcast, the one inspired by my 'all dads' conversation with Zoe. On *The Dad Kit*, I interviewed well-known Aussies like Guy Sebastian, Jock Zonfrillo, Sam Wood and Josh Pyke, asking them to open up about fatherhood in the modern era. My hope was to change the national narrative around fatherhood, one conversation at a time. I didn't realise how profoundly the podcast would change me.

Marc Fennell had won every international award in every category for every media type that existed, and that made me equal parts jealous and impressed. I didn't actually know a lot about his personal life, other than the pictures I'd seen on Instagram of his two kids, but I asked my producer to reach out anyway. Marc accepted rather quickly, and we met up in person a few weeks later.

Our chat was wonderful. Marc opened up about his relationship with his father and the struggles he had throughout his own parenting journey, and the end of the conversation really stuck with me. The final question I asked every guest was, 'What do you think it means to be a good dad?' Marc paused and said it couldn't 'be boiled down to one single thing', but he found it helpful to recognise 'that you're a support player in their story'. He explained that 'It does become easier as they get older and they start to look like protagonists in their own story. As they've gotten older, they have so much more personality and they demonstrate interest in things. I've found the most effective thing for me is to fall in line with that.' He described his children's interests, spoke passionately about supporting them, and said he felt most comfortable in spaces where he could do that.

Perhaps just as an afterthought, Marc concluded, 'What I think I probably need to work more on is working out where the Venn diagrams overlap. What would be lovely is, as they get older, to find really clear overlaps where we can enjoy things together. Finding the spaces in the Venn diagrams between what you love and what they love and things you can invest in together. Because my dad and I are not super close, but the things I remember are the things that sat in the Venn diagram between his interest and what soon became mine.'

While it's possible that Marc has never thought about the interview again, I have never forgotten those last four sentences – in fact, I've become a disciple of the religion that is Marc Fennell's Venn Diagram Approach to Parenting.

In the weeks after that interview, I took a trip down memory lane, and his approach came into sharp focus for me. As I looked back at my childhood, almost all of the positive memories that floated to the top included activities that both my parents and I loved: cooking, sewing and crafting with my mother, and building things, eating sushi, listening to music, and vintage shopping with my dad. When we'd done these things together, we'd all been happy, and that had made the memories happier.

I began to wonder what it might look like to eliminate as many things that I didn't enjoy as possible from the day-to-day parenting grind, while finding as many mutually enjoyable activities as possible. If I worked towards that, would I enjoy parenting more, and would my children form stronger, happier core memories? I started to perceive all the situations where we were living far outside the centre of our Venn diagram. My mind sprinted down a long list of things I did with my children where I sat in discomfort and therefore was a pretty shitty parent.

Going to the playground, for example, made my blood boil – dirty equipment, bratty kids, uncomfortable conversations with parents I didn't want to talk to, sand and trash and pigeons, oh my! Instead of taking a break, I would push the kids on a swing for what felt like a million hours or chase them around playing monsters; if I'd wanted to run a marathon, then I'd have bloody well signed up for one. In short, I hated the playground, yet I was spending four to eight hours a week there because, well, kids like playgrounds. I was tense and uncomfortable, and couldn't wait to get home. Just because I felt like I was supposed to, I was placing my children in an environment where their father was unhappy, which meant we were definitely not creating positive core memories together.

I asked myself what other play-centric environments I might enjoy more. I found indoor play centres, local beaches, walking trails and swimming pools, and took the twins to them much more often, allowing Josh to step in and become Playground Dad. The result? Happier fathers, happier children.

But I didn't stop there: I asked myself which of my interests the twins might enjoy too. First, I started watching tennis with them. In the mornings, when I would watch highlights from overnight matches, I'd ask Stella and Cooper to sit on my lap. Stella took a liking to Ash Barty, Naomi Osaka and Coco Gauff, then she asked for a tennis racquet for her birthday and began taking lessons.

Next, I drew pictures with the kids. We started by focusing on letters and simple shapes, but our sketches quickly evolved to cat faces and love hearts and stars. Cooper developed a passion for drawing. Every morning when I woke up, he was already at the living-room table creating an intricate zoo map; every night before dinner, he begged us to let him draw for a few more minutes.

I then tried introducing the twins to one of my greatest passions: drag queens.

*

My second year at college, I auditioned for the school's dance company and was cast as Carmen Miranda in the Jazz & Tap Company production of *Puttin' on the Ritz*.

'What does this mean?' I asked my professor and the company's choreographer, Gay Nardone.

'You know who Carmen Miranda is, right?' she asked.

'The Spanish dancer with all that fruit on her head?'

'You will be playing her. I think you're perfect for it.'

'No, no, no,' I blurted without thinking, forgetting who I was talking to. 'Wear a dress? I can't do that – my dad will be in the audience.'

She laughed, certain I was joking. After all, I had a reputation for confident feminine expression. I mostly danced in booty shorts, and whenever Gay taught gendered dance moves to the class, I exclusively performed the woman's part without asking for permission. It wasn't far-fetched for my professor to think I'd be comfortable in the role of Carmen. But while I would have been jealous if another man had been given the role, I couldn't unpick my discomfort about dancing in heels and a dress in front of thousands of people.

Gay was a mother figure to me back then, balancing a tough-love communication style with warmth and empathy. As a Radio City Rockette, she'd toured the world with some of the best tap dancers alive, so I had a great deal of respect for her. When she tapped, I was laser-focused on her feet; when she spoke, I listened. She knew this all too well.

'When I was your age,' she said to me, shortly after my outburst, 'I was excited to be given a part at all. So many girls were getting cut every few hours, so when they said, "You're going to be a reindeer in the show," I smiled and became the reindeer.'

My anxiety had momentarily caused me to lose sight of the bigger picture. I was a performer with over a decade of both amateur and professional experience, and I had never walked into an audition room demanding or even expecting a role – the goal had always been just to get cast. How was this situation any different? It was time for me to grow up and leave my fear of judgement – from strangers and even my own father – outside the rehearsal hall.

I gave it my all as Carmen. After a few rehearsals, I'd forgotten the anxiety over being seen as 'too gay' or 'wanting to be a woman', and replaced it with anxiety over learning how to dance in heels, something I'd never done before. I soon became consumed with leaping, kicking and pirouetting in three-inch red dancer heels. And like with every other role I'd been given, I lost myself in the character. I asked myself, 'What would

Here I am in all my Carmen Miranda glory. Photo courtesy of University of New Hampshire.

Carmen do here? Would she wink or show some leg? Is she flirting with a boy in the audience at this point, or connecting with her girlfriends on stage? What's my intention as I bend backwards at the end of the number and stare the audience members in the eye?' I chose – much like the drag queen I'd judged back at Club 313 – to be confident in what I brought to the table.

A couple of years later, I was cast as Angel in *Rent*. This time, I was thrilled when the cast list was announced and showed up to rehearsal ready to learn. It was during that production that I truly fell in love with drag as an art form.

The director brought in a professional drag queen from a neighbouring town to teach me how to glue down my brows, paint my face, rhinestone my lips, and style Angel's various wigs. Sitting in that makeup chair was where I first learned about *RuPaul's Drag Race*. The show, only in its second season, hadn't gained international or even national recognition yet. According to my drag queen stylist, it was mostly a show for other drag queens. I didn't watch it then, but I googled the cast and was pleased to see they were a variety of different shapes and sizes, with a variety of aesthetics and skill sets: some could dance, some could sing, some were 'look queens' on the runway, and some cracked jokes better than stand-up comedians.

I now knew first-hand that drag queens weren't just doing basic makeup: they were creating illusions with paint, hiding masculine features and transforming their faces. They weren't just throwing on wigs: they were layering three or four on top of each other and styling them with fourteen cans of hairspray.

They were also designing and sewing their own high-fashion runway costumes, choreographing their own dances, and memorising a few new songs each week while ensuring their lip-syncing matched up perfectly. They had to command a stage with improv and top-tier comedy, engage with audiences of various kinds, and deal with trolls as they managed their social media presence.

The more I thought about it, the more impressed I became. Drag queens were fabulous, committed, brave actors developing larger-than-life characters. Each performance was a rebellious 'fuck you' to the cisheteronormative structures that had bound us as queer boys. I didn't want to do it myself, but I fell head over heels for what drag represented.

*

I typed 'Best Drag Race Lip Syncs' into YouTube and played the first video that popped up: an eleven-minute montage edited and uploaded by a user named That RPDR Channel. Unlike all the previous times I'd watched a drag clip around my children, I decided to play it loudly enough for them to hear.

As soon as Demi Lovato's 'Sorry, Not Sorry' began blaring from my phone, Stella stopped colouring in her unicorn book and turned to face me. 'Can I watch that with you?'

'Of course you can!' I replied, impressed that my plan had worked so quickly.

'What are those girls doing?' Stella asked as she pushed her way onto my lap, leaving Cooper, who seemed uninterested, colouring on the floor.

'Those aren't girls. Those are boys who dress up as girls for a job.'

'They look like girls!'

'That means they're doing a good job, because that's their goal.'

'But I don't think I like this video.'

'That's okay,' I said, as my heart sank a little. 'You don't have to watch it.' Maybe this would be an activity that remained solely on my side of the Venn diagram. 'But we could watch another one and see if you like that one better?'

'Another one, another one!' she cheered.

I fast-forwarded to the third performance, skipping over a dance that I knew had inappropriate moves. I landed on Alyssa Edwards and Tatianna lip-syncing to 'Shut Up and Drive' by Rihanna.

As the video began to play, Stella sat in silence. Then she said, 'I wish I could do that,' as the performers made synchronised leaps.

'Well, you can. You can take dance lessons.'

'I want to take dance lessons. I want to take ballet.'

'Alyssa,' I said, gesturing to her on the screen, 'is a professional dance teacher.'

'I want to be a dance teacher, too!' Stella announced. Then the fourth video began, and she was drawn to one of the performers. 'Who is that?' she asked, pointing.

'That's Denali,' I said.

'I like what she is wearing. She looks like a bird.'

'It's supposed to be like a bird – a toucan, I think. And doesn't she dance amazingly? She's a professional choreographer!'

'What is a coro-grapher?'

'A choreographer is the person who comes up with dance moves.'

'I want to be a choreographer!'

'Well, taking dance lessons is a really good place to start.'

'And I want to dress up as a bird!'

'Okay.' I laughed, loving how excited she was becoming. 'We can find you a bird costume.'

When that clip ended, I began to close my laptop. As far as I was concerned, I had shared something with my daughter that brought me great joy, and she didn't hate it – that, on its own, was a massive win.

'Can we watch it again?' Stella asked, sticking her hand into the laptop before I could finish closing it.

'Of course we can. You like it?'

'I love, love, love, love, love it!' she said with a massive smile.

So we sat there together, watching Denali's lip-sync performance on repeat for close to thirty minutes.

The truth is, Stella doesn't love or hate drag queens, and she's too young to watch most of the performances in *Drag Race*. But she knows they exist, and she knows her dada loves them. Cooper does, too, but he's never been interested in the same way as Stella. Every few weeks, she asks if we can watch the 'toucan coro-grapher', and I excitedly race to play the video. Cooper pokes his head over her shoulder every now and then, sees what we're watching and just says 'drag queen' or 'toucan' before disappearing back to his drawings.

Sharing your side of the Venn diagram with your kids, confidently opening up and showing them the things you love, makes it easier to find out what overlaps with their side. I want my kids to have access to me in totality. I want them to understand the various shades of my personality. I want to set the stage for them to share in passions of mine as these become age-appropriate. And I want to, if possible, create positive core memories together by finding mutual passions.

Chapter Twenty-two

The Label

My children are bisexual.

They're only five years old, so I know what you're thinking: they're a little young. But I don't mean that I've imposed a sexual orientation on them – I just mean that their father and I decided early on to create a space free from assumptions about sexuality.

Josh and I first joked about the idea long before we became dads. In fact, the topic was broached before we'd even moved in together, in late 2011.

'I hate that everyone treats straightness as if it was the only option,' I told him. 'I've hated it my entire life.'

'In what types of situations?' Josh replied.

'All of them, really. But mostly in small talk. Every chance a guy gets to bring up a girlfriend or a potential girlfriend or an ex-girlfriend, he uses it. It's just this constant stream of straightness that's always being pushed my way.'

'Pushed everyone's way,' he agreed. 'But if everyone had said "boyfriend" or "husband" to you – back in high school, for example – that wouldn't have made it better, would it?'

'Fair point. I hated people trying to out me, especially before I really had proof that I liked boys. It's a lose-lose, I guess.'

'We should do away with sexuality,' Josh announced. 'It shouldn't be an assumption.'

I laughed. 'That's ridiculously good!'

'Just leave it ambiguous for kids until they tell you.'

'It eliminates closets and the need for coming out of them. It's brilliant.'

We ordered another round of martinis and raised a toast to our bisexual-unless-proven-otherwise unborn children.

★

I was driving the twins to preschool when, seemingly out of the blue, Stella asked to hold my wedding ring.

'I can't actually take it off.' I pulled up at a red light, and there was just enough time for me to twist around, hold my hands out to the kids and attempt to tug the ring from my chubby finger. The action was destined to fail: the only way I could remove the tungsten and koa wood band, the one I'd not-so-subtly demanded Josh purchase for me, was with lubricant – and we didn't keep that in the car.

'Do you never take it off?' Cooper chimed in.

The light went green, and I kept driving. 'I never take it off, no. Not for the last eight years. I don't want to. If you look at my skin under the ring, you can see a totally different colour. I like to look at it every now and then.'

'Why?' Stella asked.

'It's a reminder of the past, and—'

She pounced. 'The past?'

'Yeah, the past is anything that happened before this moment. The present is this car ride, and the past is everything that happened before we got in the car. When I look at the pale skin under the ring, it's a little reminder of who I was before I met your daddy.'

'What's a reminder?' Cooper asked, through a mouth packed full of apple pieces.

'It's, um, a thing that causes you to remember something. Like your toy snake makes you think of Abuela and Papa coming to visit last month. It's a *reminder* of that time you spent together. Does that make any sense?'

'No,' he replied honestly. He rolled down his window and shoved the face of his black rubber snake out of it.

Before I could dive into a further explanation for him, Stella grabbed back the reins of the wedding conversation. 'Will I get married one day?' she screamed over the sound of the wind now pouring into the car.

'If you want to,' I yelled, then checked that Cooper had withdrawn his snake from the window before rolling it up so she could hear me. 'It's totally up to you – you don't have to get married!'

'When will I get married?' she asked without skipping a beat.

'That's up to you, too. It's something adults do, so you have some time to think about it. But usually adults get married when they're in their late twenties or in their early thirties like Dada. But some people wait until they are in their forties or fifties or sixties.'

'How old were you and Daddy?'

'I was twenty-six and Daddy was thirty-six.'

'Who will *I* get married to?' she asked, ignoring our meaningless ages.

It was clear then that my daughter was on a fact-finding mission. Although she'd asked for my personal details, they were of little interest to her. She wanted a wedding ring, and she wasn't going to stop asking questions until she knew if and when she would receive one, and who exactly would be placing it on her finger.

'That's up to you, too.' I giggled, annoyed at myself – only slightly – for the repetitive nature of my responses. 'If you find a person you really love, then you two will decide together if marriage is something you want to do.'

'Do I have to marry a man like Daddy?' Stella asked.

'No, you can marry whoever you want, or no one at all. You don't have to get married if you don't want to. If you do want to, your spouse definitely doesn't have to be like Daddy. But hopefully they are kind like Daddy.'

'But how will I know?' Her tone shifted from youthful curiosity to mature concern.

'Do you mean, how will you know they are kind?' I asked.

'No – that I want to get married!'

'You'll just feel it inside.' I took my eyes off the road to catch her gaze in the rear-view mirror. 'Like there's no other option in the world.'

Stella smiled and then stared out the window, probably daydreaming about that perfect person popping a perfect ring on her perfect finger.

Speaking of perfect, I had to share another photo of Stella and Cooper at this age.

The Label

★

I treated my kids as bisexual a few weeks later, too. We'd just arrived home from preschool, and I was making a smoothie while they watched Disney's *Brave* for the fifteenth time that month. I was elbow-deep in frozen mixed berries when Cooper sprinted into the kitchen and asked, 'Can I get pregnant?'

'No, you can't have a baby in your belly because you need a uterus for that. But you can still be a father, like me. Why, buddy?'

'Because Stella said—'

Cooper was interrupted by his boisterous sister, who screamed at the top of her lungs from across the house, 'I can have a baby because I'm a girl!'

'That's almost right.' I peeked out of the kitchen and met her gaze. '*Most* girls can have babies.'

Stella got up and came to join us in the kitchen. 'I can get pregnant right now.' She grabbed her belly with both hands and applied pressure, as if she could force her tummy to swell by sheer will.

'No, no. Not yet, sweetie.' I laughed. 'You have to get your period first, remember?'

'And *then* I will get pregnant?'

'Then you probably *can* get pregnant. But it doesn't just happen. You need …' I paused to collect my thoughts, hoping to nail the explanation on the first go so I wouldn't say the wrong thing and accidentally scar her for life. 'You would need help.'

'What kind of help?' she asked.

I took a deep breath, zipped up a bag of frozen berries and kneeled in front of her, pulling Cooper in closer.

This felt like a huge parenting moment, one for the record books. I had naively imagined I wouldn't need to have this conversation for another few years, so I wasn't as prepared as I would have liked. But here we were. I needed to give an honest answer.

'That's a very good question. Most women have tiny eggs in their belly, remember that? And most men have tiny seeds inside their testicles, called sperm.'

'What's a testicle?' Stella asked.

Cooper giggled. 'The balls.'

'That's right, buddy, very impressive. You need eggs and sperm to combine if you want to make a baby. When two grown-ups love each other, they can make a baby together, or a doctor can help to make a baby for them. That's what Dada and Daddy did.'

'So I can marry a woman and have a baby?' Stella asked, smiling.

'Sure you can.' I smiled back.

'But I will marry a woman and have a baby with her,' said Cooper.

'That's lovely. It doesn't matter who you fall in love with, or even if you never fall in love with someone – if you want to have kids, there should be a way.'

A couple of days after that, I treated my kids as bisexual again. Our neighbour was talking to Stella about school formals. 'In a fancy dress, you'll go to a dance with a boy–'

'Or a girl!' I said.

The Label

★

I was thirteen years old and hanging out with my good friend Sarah – not to be confused with Sara, our surrogate – at her place one evening before our Jazz Funk class. I felt very comfortable with Sarah, who had taken me under her wing from my first day at middle school. She was the smart kid who wasn't afraid to push back and ask questions in class, which made me in total awe of her.

That evening, we hid from her 'annoying' little sister and found ourselves in her closet. We listened to music and huddled together beneath her clothes, reading the names of cute boys at school that she had scribbled on the closet wall.

I, too, had a crush on one of them. I felt safe and I was so sick of lying. Without thinking, I felt the words pour from my mouth. 'Matt is so cute.'

I froze. I had just outed myself in a closet. Luckily I was certain that Sarah, of all people, wouldn't care. She was much more mature than the other kids in our grade, a step ahead of the rest. But I had zero experience communicating with someone about this, so I remained silent and kept staring at the names.

'Do you like boys?' Sarah asked without judgement.

I paused, unsure how to respond. I had never actually spoken the words into existence. But I knew that I liked boys. I had already acted on my attraction several secret times, kissing them and exploring their nether regions at sleepovers, pool parties and church retreats. I was also knee-deep in my nightly ritual of praying the gay away, so I believed there was still hope God would miraculously change me. If I admitted to Sarah that I was gay, or bisexual as my safer option, there might be no turning back. Most importantly, admitting this to Sarah would mean admitting it to myself. The moment it happened, it would be real. And the moment it was real, my life would surely be over.

'I think so,' I said. 'But I like girls, too. Please don't tell anyone.'

'It's okay,' she said. 'I won't. I think I like girls and boys, too.'

'Have you acted on it?' I blurted out. I was desperate to admit to someone I trusted that I had been sinning and loving every minute of it; that it felt natural and freeing and far from wrong.

'A little. You know, at a sleepover. Just kissing and stuff. Have you?'

'Yeah, me too.'

I felt instant relief, the first of many shoulder drops when some of the pressure lifted off. I had just come out with fifty per cent of the truth, and it hadn't blown up in my face. This seemed a step in the right direction.

Sarah's mom called for us, letting us know our dance class would start soon. When we emerged from that closet, we were still closeted. In that bedroom, we left our truth. We looked at each other as if to say, 'This was a big deal', and then we, unfortunately, didn't speak about it again.

Many years later, I invited Sarah to my wedding. I couldn't celebrate the greatest achievement of my life without having the first person I came out to in the audience.

When I addressed our friends and family that day, I said, 'I never thought this moment would happen. I never thought this would be possible, not for someone like me.'

The Label

I was scanning the audience, doing my best to remain calm, but then my eyes locked with Sarah's. I just lost it, tears streaming down my face.

'There was a time when I never even allowed myself to imagine this level of happiness, yet here we are.' I was speaking for that thirteen-year-old boy in that closet. He had been willing to admit some of the truth, but he hadn't believed it was good, and he hadn't believed it meant he could have a happy life. And now he did.

★

Stella was getting married, and all the toys in the house were invited. Cooper wasn't interested in marriage, which I really couldn't argue with.

Earlier that day, I had found myself having to explain my journey to Gayville to Stella and Cooper for the first time. The three of us were sitting side by side in their playroom on a large IKEA rug. We were all in fancy dress and Stella had a white tea towel draped over her head to mimic a wedding veil.

'Have you ever been married to a girl?' my daughter asked.

'No, only to Daddy. But I've been in relationships with girls.'

'What's that?'

'Good question. It's when you have a very special bond with someone. When two people decide they want to be together, to see if they might grow to love each other, people call that a romantic relationship or dating. So I dated girls before I met Daddy.'

'Did you want to marry them?' she asked.

'Hmmm … I definitely loved them. But, no, I didn't want to marry them. I didn't love them the same way I love Daddy. Not the same way I've loved boys.'

'You love boys the most?' Cooper jumped in.

'Yes, I love boys the most.'

'What if I love boys the most?' Stella asked.

'What do you mean?'

'Will you be mad?'

'No, of course not, my love. You can love whoever you want to love and be whoever you want to be. Daddy and I do not care at all – we just want you to be happy.'

'And if I love girls and boys, what is that?'

'People call that "bisexual". But you don't have to worry about that. Just focus on being a kid, and listen to your heart as you grow.'

'I like girls and boys,' Stella proudly announced.

'I just like girls,' said Cooper, just as proudly.

'That's fantastic,' I said, rubbing their cheeks at the same time. 'Thank you for telling me. And if it changes, you can tell me that too – even if it changes a million times.'

'I'd like to get married,' Stella said with a smile.

'Then maybe you will one day, when you're a bit older–'

'I'd like to get married today.'

'To whom? I didn't know you were dating anyone. Five is a bit young to get married, don't you think?'

'To Piper and to Dog.'

'Your stuffed animals?'

'Yes, a big wedding.' She lifted her toy puppies off the carpet and held them to her cheeks, grinning up at me. 'Piper is a girl, and Dog is a boy.'

'Oh, of course. How silly of me. Well, then we'd better start planning for the big event. We've got no time to waste.'

I texted Josh: *We're throwing a big bisexual wedding tonight when you get home from work.*

He texted back: *Who ... the children?*

Yep, I replied.

Huh. Are the toys involved?

You bet.

On my phone, the text-message dots flickered as he typed. *Sit tight. I'll bring cake.*

Chapter Twenty-three

The 'They'

It was well and truly past midnight, and I just couldn't sleep. I lay there in our bed, three hours after crawling into it, staring up at the ceiling fan. Its soft, irregular hum was in near-perfect unison with the warm breaths of my husband. The heel of my right foot was cramping because I'd been practising a ballet pointe after years of neglect.

At 9 am, my daughter would be taking her first ballet class. Every time I thought about Stella walking into the studio dressed in her adorable little costume, I felt equal parts warm nostalgia for my childhood, hopefulness that she wouldn't hate dancing, and an unavoidable fear that she might actually like it, maybe as much as I did. And then, perhaps, she'd wake up decades later with a broken heart and torn muscles.

I couldn't help worrying that I was encouraging her to take these classes because I wanted to find my way back into a dance studio, my happy place.

The 'They'

Earlier that evening, I'd laid out her costume on the floor of her bedroom: a pink Flo Dancewear leotard with ruffled sparkly sleeves, a matching pair of prima pink tights and her slippers. Next to them, I'd placed a collection of hair accessories to make a ballet bun: a brush, a hand mirror, hairspray, bobby pins, and elastics that matched her hair colour. I knew how to make a bun – I'd spent nearly two decades surrounded by girls preparing for class – but the excitement overcame me and I felt I had no choice but to watch a few hours of YouTube tutorials to ensure it was perfect.

Sure, this was just her introductory class. And yeah, she was only five. But this was the only way I knew how to dance: a hundred per cent commitment or nothing at all.

At 5.30 am, I awoke to my daughter's hand stroking my arm. 'I have ballet class soon,' she whispered.

'Yes, you do.'

'Can you wake up and make me breakfast?'

'I'm up, baby girl. I'll meet you downstairs soon and help you get into your outfit.'

'I'm already in it,' she said.

I wiped the crust from my eyes and properly opened them to see my daughter fully dressed and prepared for class. It seemed that Stella had chosen a hundred per cent commitment. The apple, or maybe mango in this case, hadn't fallen far from the tree.

Josh and I had asked Cooper if he wanted to dance too, but his response was simple: 'No, I want to do karate.' So we'd signed him up for a Thursday class, glad to give the twins a chance to enjoy separate activities of their choosing. I wasn't keen on forcing my son to do an activity against his will just to relive my childhood *Billy Elliot* fantasy.

While Cooper and Josh got ready for the day, Stella and I sat in front of a large circular mirror while I did her hair.

'Are you excited?' I asked, staring at her reflection.

'Yes! Very excited!'

'Good. Just remember, this is a test class. If you don't like it, we don't ever have to go again, no pressure. This is supposed to be fun, you know. You don't have to take dance class for me. I don't care if you dance, you kn—'

'I know that, Dada.' She looked up at me with suspicion.

We'd never once spoken about Stella doing this for me, so my insistent rambling had come out of nowhere for her. In fact, she had decided to take ballet after watching drag videos with me. But when her confused eyes met my own, I realised I'd been trying to convince myself.

*

I started playing American football in the 8th Grade, in hopes of getting even closer to my father. There wasn't anything wrong with our relationship – like I've said, he was a loving and supportive parent. But I knew he was closer with my siblings in a particular way, and that knowledge chipped away at my self-esteem.

My family was very athletic. My parents had been college athletes – my dad played lacrosse, my mom basketball – and physical prowess had seeped down into the next generation. By the time I was fifteen, I had swum competitively, gone sailing, played baseball, soccer, lacrosse, tennis and golf, and done track and field as well as gymnastics. But even though I'd become a top-tier competitive dancer, capable of jumping off a platform into a split, I never felt athletic enough ... not as athletic as my siblings, that is.

Whenever my brother and sister and I fought, like all good siblings should, my sportiness was brought into question. They knew, bless their competitive hearts, that it was a sore spot. I was the dancer in a family of lacrosse players, the flamboyant black sheep. While that didn't have a huge impact on my confidence on the dance floor – this black sheep loved applause – it did mean I spent less time with my father than my siblings did. As I got older, that really started to bother me.

If I wanted to extend my time with Dad outside of car rides and movie nights, I had two choices: play lacrosse or play football. Lacrosse seemed like the obvious route. I was comfortable with the stick – he'd literally put one in my hand when I was a few days old – and I knew I could throw and catch the ball, having played with my siblings growing up. So I signed up for a lacrosse summer camp in 7th Grade, run by my father and a few other local dads. But I was paired with my worst school bully, who wiped the balls so hard in my direction, I spent most of the practice running down the hill to retrieve them. When asked if I wanted to return, I politely declined – or maybe I screamed at the top of my lungs after slamming my bedroom door. It's hard to remember. Either way, it was clear I had to try football, even though it was the straightest of all sports, and I was, well, the gayest of all kids.

My dad coached football, my brother played football, and my sister was a cheerleader at football games. Each weekday the rest of my family was at the field for practices, with my mom preparing snacks and drinks, so chucking another Gallerani into the mix made sense. When my parents asked me if I wanted to sign up that year, I said yes.

The first practice was one of the worst physical experiences of my life. I wasn't prepared for the intensity of the workout or the coach's screams. I cried in my helmet as we ran laps around the field, vomited in my mouth after coming last in the group sprints, and pretended to have an asthma attack while running basic drills in front of the entire team.

Whenever I had a chance to think, I planned my resignation speech to my parents: 'I know we're not quitters. I know we finish things. But I'm not like those boys – I can't tackle those giants. I'm sorry for disappointing you.'

Then Trevor, the best player on the team, did something unexpected during a one-on-one drill. I ran towards him and wrapped my arms around his waist – and he tumbled to the ground. It was my first successful tackle. The team cheered, and as Trevor stood up, he gave me a friendly wink and said, 'Nice hit. Aim a bit higher next time.'

I suddenly felt like one of the boys.

I'd love to pretend I didn't care about their acceptance, but that would be a blatant lie: I was desperate for it. I had tried everything in my power to be more manly – lowering my voice, dating women, wearing baggy clothes, walking with more swagger, listening to rap music – but I had never pulled it off. My feminine energy was in my walk, my voice, my hair and my build. It had

Whenever I see the number 51 out in the wild, I have a rush of pride. I was a gay high school football player, and no one can take that away from me.

placed a division between me and more masculine guys. And it had made me, for as long as I could remember, their target.

On a football field, of all places, that invisible barrier began to chip away. I decided to go to the next practice after all, then the next one, then the next. Trevor looked after me on the field, then the coaches and some of the other players joined him.

Prior to arriving on that field, I had placed myself in a tiny queer box. I'd thought that because the world had decided I was one type of man, then maybe I was. I had started to believe I wasn't man enough; that my gayness meant I would forever sit on the sidelines watching as the straight world passed me by; that the fragile femininity expected of a 'fairy' like me meant I would only ever be accepted in dance studios, choirs and art classes.

Football taught me that I was so much more than just 'the gay guy'. Over the next couple of years, I gained confidence in a sport that the world said a boy like me didn't have a right to play. Inside of myself, I found a physical strength and connection to my masculinity that I'd never known was there. I could be gay and be one of the boys, because – contrary to popular opinion – I *was* a man, and my limp wrists, soft voice and love of dancing couldn't negate that fact.

Football also taught me that jocks weren't always nasty bullies ruining queer kids' lives. In fact, they could be the exact opposite.

One day, Trevor walked straight up to my car after practice and knocked on my window. 'I hear that you're gay,' he said as I rolled it down. 'Is that true?'

'Um … yeah.'

'That's cool. Listen, if anyone ever messes with you, come find me.'

The second he turned to walk away, waving as I rolled up the window, I dropped my head between my legs and burst into tears. *Maybe this gay thing won't ruin my high school career,* I thought. *Maybe the stereotypes about football players aren't that different from the stereotypes about gay kids.*

I still thought the way to my father's heart was through football. I imagined that when he watched me dance, he was wishing I could be more like my siblings, and that he would be much happier at one of my football games.

Then Dad found himself in a verbal altercation with another father during one of my dance recitals. At intermission, my sister filled me in. 'Someone was making fun of you, and Dad stood up for you, saying how proud he is to watch you dance.'

My narrative instantly shifted: it wasn't the sport that he loved, it was the person playing it – or not playing it. Dad didn't care about me playing lacrosse or football; he never had. I'd just been projecting my insecurities onto him. It wasn't my confidence on the field that had strengthened our bond – hell, I was terrible at football – it was the confidence the game gave me off the field.

After the dance recital, we embraced backstage as we always did. He pulled back, looked me square in the eye and said, 'I'm so proud of you.' Even though he'd said it thousands of times before, I finally heard it.

Later that week, while sitting with Dad in our kitchen, I told him I didn't want to play football anymore. I was crying, as is often the case when I'm nervous, and found myself back in his warm embrace. 'You don't have to play football,' he said. 'Not for me. I just want you to be happy.'

★

I wanted Stella to dance because I understood it inside and out. I'd grown up in a dance studio, studied dance and worked professionally as a dancer. The stretches, positions and routines were wired deep into my being. It felt normal, necessary even, to try to pass that love down to at least one of my children and bring dance into the centre of our Venn diagram.

There was another motivation, though, one I felt uncomfortable admitting to anyone in my friendship group. None of us wanted to enforce gender stereotypes, yet I was excited about Stella dancing because she was a girl, the only girl in a house of boys, the only female cousin in an Australian gang of four kids. I wanted to provide her with opportunities to connect with other girls. Without a female role model in the house, I was more conscious than the average parent of giving her access to feminine influences.

Dance isn't just for girls – I know that, obviously! – but it is taught, learned and performed predominantly by women. As a boy I had watched my female classmates learn routines, prepare for recitals and bond with one another as they dressed in their elegant tutus and pinned up their tight buns, and I wanted my daughter to experience the same thing – if she wanted to, of course.

I was raising a girl. It had never crossed my mind to think about it any other way. But societal conversations around gender had shifted, and by 2020 I now knew that it was possible that

Stella might correct me one day. That the child I saw as my daughter might grow up and feel different about or want to explore her gender identity.

I'd recently been hanging out in a dedicated group chat with two new friends, Deni Todorovic and Sandy McIntyre, both of whom I'd met on Instagram. Deni and Sandy are non-binary, and thanks to our budding friendship, I'd learnt a huge amount about gender in a very short time.

Prior to Deni coming out in 2020, I had never understood what 'non-binary' meant. A few months prior I'd read something about the British pop star Sam Smith being non-binary, but embarrassingly I hadn't looked into it much further, as it wasn't something that resonated with me personally. On Instagram I'd seen some people using they/them pronouns, but I had just thought — again, quite embarrassingly — that this had something to do with transitioning, perhaps a space someone could occupy while they explored coming out as transgender.

Thanks to Deni and Sandy, I learned that being non-binary isn't a transitional phase, but instead the gender identity of people who don't identify as a man or a woman. These people occupy a space outside the gender binary, as both male and female or as neither. It was important for me to use the correct pronouns for my new friends — and not to make too big a deal and put an emotional burden on them when I occasionally slipped up at first.

At the time, I happened to be developing a podcast called *Come Out Wherever You Are*. While doing some serious work in therapy around my coming-out experience, I'd had the idea that there would be an audience for a show where I interviewed Australian celebrities about coming out. The team at LiSTNR had gladly thrown their weight behind the show. My guests included a range of gender non-conforming legends like Courtney Act, Kath Ebbs, Allira Potter and Rudy Jean Rigg – plus Deni and Sandy, of course.

*

I had put in the hours, done the research, spoken with non-binary people and internally worked through my own issues with gender. So when my very best friend, Joe, came out to me as non-binary during a video chat, I felt prepared.

I paused for a second, took a deep breath and smiled softly, knowing this was one of those rare opportunities to respond in the way I wished people had responded back when I came out. 'It's so nice to finally meet you,' I said, as tears fell from their eyes. 'I'm honoured that you trust me with this news, and I can't wait to get to know you even better.'

Shortly after Joe came out to me, I sat my children down to explain what 'non-binary' meant. I had already shown them pictures of Deni and Sandy on my phone, always using the proper pronouns and doing my best to explain that these people weren't, as the twins often said, 'boys in makeup'. But Stella and Cooper were old enough now that I felt confident they could handle a more serious conversation about gender.

Joe had been a massive part of my life ever since we met in 2006. Over the course of the next decade, they had become my chosen family. They were the only guest who attended all three

This is the first photo that Jo and I took together at our university prom. After that night, we became inseparable.

of my weddings. So it was important that my children knew to respect their pronouns.

'You know Uncle Joe, right?'

'Yes,' Cooper replied, while Stella said, 'The one with the pretty makeup.'

'That's right. Well, Joe is non-binary. Some people, like Dada and Daddy, are boys. And some people, like Nanna, are girls. But other people, like Joe, aren't girls or boys. They're not one or the other.' I was trying to introduce the concept quickly and easily so the twins would maintain their focus and be able to understand. 'When we talk about Joe, we don't say "he". Instead, we say "they" or "them". Like this: "*They* are beautiful. Look at *them* wearing makeup." Does that make sense?'

They both nodded and said, 'Yes!'

'Do you have any questions?' I asked them.

'Can we watch *Bluey* now?' Stella said.

'Please?' Cooper said.

This wasn't the passionate engagement I had hoped for, but it was a start. I was working towards educating my children about how to respect my very best friend in the world. And that, even if they'd been preoccupied by *Bluey*, was a proud parenting moment for me.

Two weeks later, Stella was drawing a picture of Joe on a piece of paper at the dining table. Joe had been exploring makeup since their transition, and Stella was fascinated with their beauty. She loved drawing their face, mohawk and all, then using all the colours of the rainbow to add elaborate designs.

'That's gorgeous, Stella,' I said. 'Is that Joe?'

'Yes, can't you tell?'

'I can. Let me take a picture and send it to him.'

'Them.'

'What?' I said.

'Send it to *them*.'

And just like that, the student had become the teacher.

The Epilogue

For most of my life I hated being gay. I hated it when I sat in the church pews as a kid and looked up at Jesus on the cross, knowing I had failed him and God. I hated anxiously waiting to come out to my parents in the middle of the night. I hated it when bullies called me names, and my uncle said I was a 'sinner', and I had to lie to girlfriends so people would think I was straight. I hated it when kids at school used the word 'gay' to mean 'uncool', and when they tortured my brother behind my back. I hated it when I couldn't see myself reflected in the media I watched or the music I listened to. I hated it when I had to sneak around with closeted men just to experience the rush of physical contact.

Even after learning to love my gayness, I still struggled. Like when I fell in love with Josh but marriage equality wasn't legal, and when we travelled the world together but I was too afraid to hold his hand in public. It annoyed me on my wedding day when a guest said, 'I never thought I'd come to one of these gay weddings', and one of the wedding cards said, 'To you and your friend.' It stressed me out it when the delivery nurse told me she'd never worked with a couple like us before. I didn't like it when strangers expected me or Josh to have a wife, without considering that two men might have children together. I hated it when women wouldn't let me into their mothers' group. And it killed me when my daughter said, 'I wish I had a mum.'

I wouldn't have told you all of that, not back then. I would have pretended I loved every aspect of being gay. It probably seemed like I was extremely comfortable with it all. But I was pushing the truth down into the bottom of my stomach, where it sat alongside decades of internalised homophobia. I hot-glued a mask of flamboyant confidence onto my face, making everyone think I was fine with this homosexual handicap – but not just fine, because that wouldn't have sufficed, now would it? I felt like I needed to make it clear I was obsessed with being gay. I'd lean against the stereotypes, make fun of myself so everyone knew I could handle a joke, turn the volume down on my voice, hit the mute button on my personality, and position myself as one of the 'cool gays', not like the others who 'rub it in your face'.

You get used to being a second-class citizen fighting for a seat at the table. You pretend it's no big deal to have your rights up for debate. You don't even bat an eye that your existence and your relationships and your right to parent are hot topics that divide families and nations alike.

I didn't like being gay. It was more annoying than the pimples on my nose and the mole on my little toe and the bags under my eyes that won't go away no matter how many creams

I apply. I felt that being gay was one of the most difficult and stressful additions to my life. But then I turned thirty-two.

★

In February 2021, I was in a bookshop in Balmain. I'd never considered myself a 'reader' per se, but I had transitioned to sleeping without my phone in our bedroom and was trying to read books each night with Josh.

I asked the woman behind the counter if she had any 'gay' books.

'Pardon me?' she said, genuinely concerned that I was being homophobic.

'I'm looking for books about queer people.'

'Sorry, of course. Let me take a look for you.' She typed for a moment, then said, 'We have *Call Me by Your Name* – you know, the one that was made into the movie with Timothée Chalamet.'

'I've actually already read that,' I said. 'Do you have anything else? Maybe a book about queer parenting?'

'It looks like we don't really have anything other than a few pride-friendly children's books. But we can order whatever you'd like. Do you have any titles in mind?'

I didn't, and I was embarrassed by that fact. I'd kind of been hoping there would be a queer section at the bookstore, with a few titles that might grab my attention. I walked out empty-handed.

That uncomfortable exchange lit a fire under my ass. I was going to find an answer to that question. I was determined to lose myself in queer literature and be the type of person who did have gay titles in mind – the type of person who knew exactly what kind of book a store could order to cater to their queer clientele. I did some research and ordered a few books online to jumpstart my Year of the Queer. I started with *The Deviant's War, Honeybee, Giovanni's Room* and *Detransition Baby.* Then I added *Gay New York, Growing Up Queer in Australia, Find Me,* and the bestselling romance novel *Red, White & Royal Blue.* As I got lost in these books, I found that I had never been happier reading in my life. It was like I had unlocked a completely obvious treasure trove that had always existed but that I'd subconsciously avoided.

It made total sense: I was uncovering a part of my own culture. I grew up learning about being Cuban and Italian from my family; we ate the food and listened to the music and heard stories about our people on television and in movies. I knew what it meant to be Catholic, thanks mostly to the Bible. But I wasn't taught anything about queer people. We didn't have a Queer Bible. There was no queer literature on the summer reading list at school, and we certainly weren't – not then, at least – celebrating queer icons as a nation. Our history, outside of Pride Month, wasn't being celebrated. How was I supposed to learn about and fall in love with this important part of me?

Back then, I had a pretty good excuse: my mom tried to find books for me, but they were impossible to locate. However, it was now 2021. Times had changed, the internet existed and I had no more excuses. I had an adult credit card with adult money on it, and I planned on reading every book by, for or about queer people, or all of the above.

It felt as though this might be what I needed to finally fall in love with being gay. The more I read, the more I learned. And the more I learned, the more at peace I felt in a larger queer community. Devouring heterosexual literature hadn't been helping me develop a sense of belonging. As I read queer love stories and researched the history of our community, I felt more and more like the struggles I had powered through in isolation weren't simply mine. There were – if the data was correct – 800 million other queer people living all around the world, struggling with the same things I had struggled with.

I really wanted to talk about all of this with anyone who would listen. I became that annoying kid who couldn't stop talking about his newest obsession: being gay.

In my weekly video calls with Joe, who now went by Jo, we started to weave in Queer History lessons. Little by little, we gave ourselves permission to educate one another on the history we hadn't been taught in school.

'I was doing research this morning for no other reason than to have some solid replies to transphobes who think being non-binary is a trend,' I said during one of these chats.

'I like where this is going,' Jo said. 'Please continue.'

'I found these writings from ancient Egypt. They're from, like, 2000 BCE. Old as hell. The Egyptians had three different genders: male, sekhet and female, listed in that order.'

'Sek-het?' they asked.

'Yeah, a third gender. If being non-binary is a trend, it's been trending for quite some time!'

My research also inspired me to create a safe space for Mom to ask me questions about our community – questions she'd always wanted to ask but hadn't been sure if she could. Some of the best conversations we've ever had occurred in that safe space, where she was able to speak freely without fear of punishment, and I helped to educate her with empathy.

My date nights with Josh changed, too. It had been years, maybe even a full decade, since we'd spoken about our sexuality. In fact, I hadn't even known much about his coming out story. So for months, I turned our date nights into Queer Q&As.

'I know you're not gay,' I probed one evening. 'And you're not bisexual … so how about pansexual? Have you heard of that one?'

'I have, yeah.'

'That one doesn't resonate with you? Liking people regardless of sex or gender identity?'

'None of them resonate with me. "Queer" probably comes closest because it has an air of transgression, of rejecting the whole idea of tribal identity groups. But I just don't buy into labels. You know that.'

'In my defence,' I said, 'you never know what new word might bounce off a page and leave you feeling euphoric. I'm spreading the gospel according to labels.'

'Do you know what does leave me feeling euphoric?' he asked.

'Tell me more.'

'Not having a label.' He smirked.

'Then cheers to that.'

For most of our relationship, I had avoided diving deep into our gender and sexuality journey, for no other reason than I'd thought we had it covered. We were two men who fell in love –

what else is there to unpack? But it turned out there was a lot. I even invited Josh onto my podcast and recorded one of its most listened-to episodes, opening people's eyes to the existence of members of our community who aren't interested in labels – to people who wince, as Josh does, at even being called 'members of our community'.

Then there was my budding friendship with Sandy McIntyre, which grew stronger over the course of the year, becoming one of the most important relationships I've formed in my adult life. We bonded over our mutual interest in our community, sharing recommendations for queer films, books and songs. And even though Sandy wasn't a parent, we had confronting and thought-provoking conversations about raising kids.

Sandy introduced me to a whole new crew of Sydney queers, and I found myself attending more queer events that popped up around the city. As my network grew, I met transgender men and women, intersex people, and non-binary folk. I met asexual and aromantic people. I met people in non-monogamous relationships, polyamorous couples and queerplatonic partnerships. Most importantly, for me at least, I collected a growing group of queer parenting friends – on and offline. I brought them onto the podcast, and we chatted about their coming-out experiences across four seasons of the show. In 2022, *Come Out Wherever You Are* won Podcast of the Year at the Radio Today Podcast Awards.

But something was missing. There was a gap in the market and a gap in my healing process. I wanted to read stories about queer parents, but I couldn't, for the life of me, find a story that looked and sounded like my own. If you can't see yourself, it's hard to be yourself.

The Epilogue

The next step in my journey presented itself as a challenge. What would happen if you wrote the book that you wished you had growing up? A book about falling in love before it was legal to marry and going down the surrogacy path. A book that covered the euphoric highs and the troubling lows of queer parenting in a straight world. A book about parenting without a script. What would happen if you shared the lessons you learned along the way, showing the world what it's really like to raise children when you're not like other dads?

One night, while Josh was reading to the twins upstairs, I opened up a blank document and began to type. 'It all started with a teapot …'

Stacey Rolfe Photography takes a great family photo. What can I say?

Acknowledgements

I want to start off by acknowledging my children, Stella and Cooper. Without the two of you, this book would not exist. My dreams of becoming a father and a storyteller were made possible the day you were born. I hope this book and the stories found inside it make you proud. Maybe not now, because you can't read. Probably not when you're fifteen either, because you'll hate everything. But maybe when you're like, I dunno, twenty-six and can appreciate what I was trying to do by sharing our stories with the world.

I need to shout from the rooftop my love and appreciation for my husband, Josh. Many of these stories are *our* stories, which you graciously let me share from my perspective. Thank you for making endless sacrifices last year so I could write (and rewrite and rewrite) this book away from my family responsibilities. My proudest achievement in the past thirty-five years has been finding and locking you down. I hope the rest of the world will fall in love with you through these stories.

In many ways, this book is a love letter to my parents. If it wasn't for the strong foundation they gave me as a child, I'm confident I wouldn't be such a loving, caring and dedicated father. I struggled to revisit some of these memories, but my mother and father kept reminding me to 'tell the world your truth without fear'. Thank you, Mother Dearest and Popsicle. I hope this book and the many stories about you that fill its pages do justice to the wonderful parents you are.

I need to thank my 'big' brother, Steven, my little sister, Samantha, and my sister-in-law, Kayla. Many of these stories are your stories, too. Thank you for the constant love and support, long before it was popular.

I want to give a special shout-out to my goddaughter, Leah, who single-handedly scanned all the photos for the book from New Hampshire, USA.

To our egg donor, your name is not mentioned in this book as we've decided to wait to share that story until our children are older, but you are, without a doubt, one of the greatest humans I've ever met. Your selfless nature inspires me to be a better human daily. While you don't get the name credit you deserve in this book, please know that our love and appreciation for you is unlimited. Your selflessness will be felt whenever this book is read.

To my in-laws, Mary Ann and Henri, thank you for raising such a beautiful boy. Thank you for welcoming me into your lives as a third son.

There are a few people who I've written about at length in this book, stories that I've chosen to tell because of the great lessons I've learned from having you in my life. Thank you for letting me share these stories with the world, Kris Coughlin, Sara and Nate Jahn, Jen, Charli Adams, Sarah A, Eric Stephens, Zoe Marshall and Sandy McIntyre.

To Jo Meallo. Thank you for letting me share your story. For allowing me to use your deadname and old pronouns so that we could authentically show readers your complete journey. And thank you for being the most consistent and reliable friend.

I'd like to thank my publisher, Jude McGee. Thank you for finding me, believing I had a story to tell and then supporting me through the first phases of this process. The rewrite nearly killed me. But in the end, you were right. Your feedback taught me an invaluable and humbling lesson that I will take with me for the rest of my career. This book is better because of you.

I'd like to thank my editor, Kate Goldsworthy, for challenging me throughout the editing process. I'm not a very spiritual person, but I have a strange feeling that you were sent to me. I know for a fact that there couldn't have been a more perfect editor for this book.

I need to thank Rachel Cramp from HarperCollins, who joined the *Not Like Other Dads* team later in the writing process but supported me through the most challenging phases. You are unbelievable at what you do and if you hadn't picked up those weekend phone calls, this book might not have made it to print.

If it wasn't for my management team at RGM, this book wouldn't have been written. Beverley, thank you for holding my hand throughout the entire process. Thank you for letting me cry to you on all those phone calls and for supporting me when I thought I couldn't possibly finish, and thank you for being the first person to read the manuscript in full. Georgia, thank you for the constant support. I am forever grateful for being part of the RGM family.

To Mari, my beloved digital manager, thank you for moving my calendar around so many times so that I could juggle the task of writing a book while also being a professional content creator. Your constant support, in every facet of my life, made writing this book so much easier.

There were so many other people who worked to ensure that this book was a success. Each of them deserve praise and recognition. Mietta Yans, my cover designer. Rebecca Sutherland, my proofreader. Caitlin Toohey, my marketing executive. And Julia Ferracane, my publicist from Righteous PR.

To my tribe, my chosen family, my very best friends Jo, Sandy, Zoe, Topher and Kyle. Writing this book consumed me for more than a year and a half. I know that I dropped the ball as a friend a few times, but please know that having your support meant the absolute world to me, and I owe you all a few rounds of drinks.

To Sarah Pike. Without you, I wouldn't have survived adolescence. This book doesn't cover our great love story, but a future book will. I promise you that.

When I lost three chapters during a freak computer glitch, two friends – both writers – called me instantly and provided invaluable advice. I was freaking out, and you two saved me. Lauren Dubois and Scott Stuart, thank you.

To the staff at Marrickville Library and Pavilion, specifically the team at Side Story Cafe: I wrote and edited ninety per cent of this book in your halls while drinking your coffee. I cried hysterically more than forty times, confusing many of your patrons. I'd like to thank you and also apologise.

Acknowledgements

To iced lattes with almond milk (no sugar), thank you for existing. You were and will always be the liquid courage I need to write my truth.

I'd also like to thank my therapists, past, present and future. But mostly present. I'm talking to you, L.

Last but not least, I want to thank me. This was easily the hardest thing I've ever done – not a single task compares. But I sat down, day after day, and wrote. I powered through discomfort while juggling difficult schedules and raising children. For that, I am extremely proud of me. In the past, I've done a terrible job of celebrating my wins and expressing pride for my achievements. That ends today.